BLACK CURRANT
PRESS
www.blackcurrantpress.com

www.blackcurrantpress.com

KNUCKLE UP

HANDS OR THE KNIFE

written by Othir Brister

ISBN # 978-0-9903781-8-1
PUBLISHED BY BLACKCURRANT PRESS COMPANY. ALL RIGHTS RESERVED.
COPYRIGHT (C) 2020 BY Othir Brister.
ALL RIGHTS RESERVED.

EDITED BY DENISE M. JOHNSON

PRINTED IN THE U.S.A.

KNUCKLE UP HANDS OR THE KNIFE

The Warden hated him…
Officers admired him…
The Prisoners would kill for him…

A South Queens Prison Story

**Written By
Othir Brister**

TABLE OF CONTENTS

Special Dedication

Acknowledgement

Forward (Note to Self)

Preface

Introduction

Chapter 1 – The Team.............…..Shady Friends
No Stranger to Violence
Product of the Streets

Chapter 2 – Lights Out Baldy …......…............................. What's in a Man?

Chapter 3 – The Academy ………....................................Trigger Happy
Downstate Correctional
Facility

Chapter 4 – First Smell of a Prison …..................................The Approach
Sing Sing Correctional Facility
Car Pooling

Chapter 5 – Keep Lock Rec Yard......................................Officers Rec (Gotcha)
B-Block Rover
What's in a Name?
The Workouts

Chapter 6 – The Beefs ………….….................................. The Fair One (One on One)

Chapter 7 – The Fights (Day of Reckoning)........................The Persuasion
Officer Down (Code Blue)
Prison Lock Down
Outside Hospital Run

Chapter 8 – The Interrogations...Confiscation of Weapons
Arbitration

Chapter 9 – Administration Attacks ….............................… The Attorney Fights for My
Freedom

Chapter 10 – Street Talk
Chapter 11 – Dreams
Chapter 12 – Spirits, Ghosts, Strange Events

Famous Quotes

Closing Dedication

He taught me not to judge a man, because I am a man.
He desired for me to be perfect, but didn't demand it.
He prepared me for all battles.
He taught me when to stand and fight,
and when to run to live to see another day.
As a child, he taught me to win the battle and he would win the
war.
He said that the Lord was my rock and He would train my
hands for battle and my fingers for war.
He told me to abandon my fears and doubts.
He said that the fight belonged to the Lord.
He taught me to be a warrior.
He stated clearly that "If God be with me, no man can stand
against me."
GOD BE WITH YOU POP!
THANKS FOR ALL YOU'VE TAUGHT ME!
LOVE YOU ALWAYS … YOUR SON!

ACKNOWLEDGEMENT

This work is an isolated product of a single mind. I am forever grateful to those who have inspired and motivated me to write about my life experiences.

Thanks mom! Those nights you prayed kept me covered with the blood! The word Queen isn't enough to express who you are!
Thanks pop! I will always be a reflection of you! If it is true that to get to the Father, one must go through the Son, then they must come through me pop, to get to you!

Thanks wifey, my rock! You've stood by me when I was broke and should have bent; when I was at my lowest point. When all others said I couldn't, your voice echoed in my ear, "You can do anything!" It made me a better father, husband, and friend. I'm forever grateful!

Thanks to my girls! Ya'll have made me the richest man in the world! It's been a pleasure to have watched you grow, learn, and make great decisions. I am so proud to be your father! Thanks girls!

Thanks to my son, whose slingshot taught me that it was not the size of the weapon, but the size of the person's heart holding the weapon! I will always have your back!

Thanks to my brothers and sisters! Growing up with you was a learning process. It gave me what I needed to survive in these streets.

Thanks to my friends who believed that I was cut from a different cloth! Thanks for your smiles and for believing in the power of conversation.

Man is the only creature that tries to control an environment beyond his control. We were in a correctional facility - a facility that housed criminals since 1826. How were we going to control something that had stood for so long?

The streets have proven that those who try to control them are either led to their incarceration or their demise. There are those who say we run these streets, and there are those who believe that they own particular areas of the streets. Guess what? These same streets that you are proclaiming have run from north to south and east to west, and they have been here long before you were ever thought of, and will be here long after you leave.

We, as men, believe that we can control everything we do with that fifth finger, the thumb. Man was made with that extra ability to grasp. He is able to hold things that other beings are not able to. For example: He who is able to hold a firearm, be it grenade or gun, is the supreme being.

PREFACE

The sworn objective of a prison guard or correctional officer is to maintain custody, care and control of a correctional institution, but there are those who take it upon themselves, for some reason or another, to taint justice.

We all know the fight of good and evil, associating itself with good or bad, or the strong and the weak, but there's the unseen character in a person that makes it more difficult to understand why a person would commit a criminal act. We put many hours into studying the psychological and behavioristic characters of these individuals and other mind-boggling programs. We tend to label a person a criminal after he has been convicted and placed in a databank. What if I were to tell you that if it weren't for the fact that correction officers and state police work in this capacity, a great percentage of them would have tendencies towards a criminal mindset. You see, the overall view of it all has a lot to do with where you grew up. This can determine whether or not you might have criminal tendencies.

Growing up in an inner city may make you more prone to commit a crime, because you're confronted with crime more frequently than those who grew up in the suburbs. For example, I would never say that all inner city individuals are prone to criminal behavior, but many suburban individuals couldn't hold a candle up to an individual who was brought up in the mean streets of New York City, or any city for that matter.

Facts: Visit an upstate New York nursery at night, where the father and mother of an infant was raised in an inner city. You will find that their infant's sleeping patterns are much different than that of a suburban infant. The inner city infant is probably wide-awake at various times throughout the night, while the suburban infant is sleeping. The energy of the parents' metabolism in that child keeps him/her alert and ready to explore.

So, with this fast moving metabolism, it creates a need; a need to exert this energy in any way possible. For those who don't become correctional officers, or officers in any area of law enforcement, we must watch ourselves. The energy is there, but so are the criminal tendencies.

The warden hated him…
Officers admired him…
The prisoners would kill for him…

A correctional officer becomes a powerful persuasion in one of New York State's most notorious prisons. His ability to persuade prisoners into illegal fighting events, leads him into an underground fighting world – a world that he calls the fair one, or the one on one: no knives, blades or shanks, just bare knuckles.

In an environment of murderers, rapists, thieves and chain snatchers, he devised a plan to manipulate the prisoners. He soon discovers that he has acquired unknown powers and a lot of respect. If anyone had a beef with another, he was the man to see. The way he did it in the Big House was prisoner against prisoner, officer against officer or officer against prisoner. This system would set a precedence in future academics and in prisons throughout New York State.

- CHAPTER 1 -

THE TEAM

Well, there I was; hands cuffed behind my back, being led out of a notorious New York State prison. This prison, which has been around since 1826, was run by trained professionals, and I thought that I was going to be able to run it from the inside, but I was wrong. How did my arrest come about? Well, let me take it from the top.

I was a young black male who wanted to be somebody. I wanted to have power and I wanted to be respected. Jobs came and went. I'd work here and there for a while and would then leave, trying to find something more – something that would hold my interest. I lived in a high crime neighborhood in Jamaica, NY, so I was familiar with crime. I knew the coke boys, the corner boys, the robbers, the second floor boys and most of the criminals. We talked often, so there was no need to fear the neighborhood, but I still wanted to be part of something more. I hit the streets to find out what the streets had to offer. As I said, I needed power and respect. I wasn't worried about the money, because the money would eventually come, or at least I knew where to get it.

I was dating this chick on the south side, who was known by a lot of guys. I went over to see her one day and came across a couple of guys who knew her. I had to feel them out to see if they could be trusted, because that's what guys do when a chick is involved. They turned out to be all right, because they were cool. We soon became a team, a crew. Every boy's dream is to have guy friends who they can hang with and who can be trusted. They're the kind of friends who you can call at any given moment if you need help with something, and they'll run right over to assist. This crew of guys had become my true friends, my team!

The players on my team were Casino, Mint, Willie Wilkins, Wayne and Lance. They were my initial team. Mint was a cool, calm and collective guy, who didn't want any trouble, but for some reason, trouble would always find him. We used to meet on his block, in front of his house a lot of times, and his mom and pop would be arguing. He was embarrassed by their yelling, so he would tell us to move further down the block to keep us from hearing their argument. His pop was a frequent drinker and when he drank, he always wanted to hit something. His mom was a very nice person, but, unfortunately, became the punching bag. I was really too young to understand the effects of alcohol then. I couldn't understand what would make his pop want to hit the mother who gave him three lovely boys!

On one particular evening, we all went over to Mint's block and were just shooting the shit on the block, when we heard yelling coming from Mint's house. Mint, Casino and I ran to his house. We entered the front door and saw his mom in the kitchen, trying to fight his pop off. He was swinging at her as if she was a punching bag. He was drunk once again! All of a sudden, something snapped in Mint. I don't know if he felt a sense of bravery with us by his side or what, but he jumped in between his parents and began swinging at his pops. He socked him real good and hit him so hard that he staggered and fell to the floor. His pops tried to get up, but Mint kept swinging at him. Casino and I couldn't do anything, because we were in shock! We were like, "What the fuck just happened?" Mint continued to swing at him. His pops realized that this was the wrong day for him to have hit his wife. You could tell that by the 'help me' look he had in his eyes. Mint eventually dragged him through the living room, out the front door, down the stairs and into the street! We had never seen Mint this upset before! He had definitely had enough of his pop's abusive ways. Casino and I watched as Mint continued to put a beating on his pops. We actually began to feel sorry for his pops, but we didn't intervene. Mint was our boy and we felt his pain; a hurt for one was a hurt for all. After a while, Mint stopped swinging at him. I guess his arms got tired. We were glad that he had stopped, because he was laying in the street on his back, on the hot cement, helpless, so we knew that his pops couldn't take any more of the blows. Mint probably would have killed him if a weapon were around. Mint was definitely out of character this day! He had never shared with us how long the abuse had been going on, but Mint sure put an end to it on that day!

There was another occasion when Mint flipped. His girl felt she needed to fool around on him, so she went out with another guy. She should have known better, because we heard talk of it in the streets. She knew that we hung in the streets with Mint, and that he was bound to find out, but didn't seem to care. Mint lost his mind when he heard about it! We also heard that the guy who she was seeing had her smoking angel dust and that she was presently on the sub-roof of her house, threatening to jump off. We hauled our asses to her house and there she was, as high as a kite, walking back and forth on her roof, talking out of her head and threatening to jump. The three of us sprang into action. Mint snuck upstairs and went close to the windowsill, while we distracted her by talking to her. We were pretty good negotiators. Mint managed to sweet talk her from the roof, and she soon climbed back inside the window. We now had to go and look for Mr. Angel Dust. We went to hang out on our favorite street corner, and we were in luck, because a few hours later, just before dark, he came prancing around that very corner. He had picked the wrong day to be walking so carefree in the streets! When we saw him, we all looked at each other as if to say, 'Who wants to go first?' Mint turned around, without saying a word, and began swinging on the dude, just like he did his pops. He swung again and again, hitting him several times in his face. I remember saying to myself, 'This dude is tough. What happened to him? He didn't even put up a fight. He would normally give you a stank face when you passed him in the streets, but not today. Casino and I watched as Mint ministered that bad a.. whipping on him. Then Mint turned to us and asked if we wanted to get some punches in as well. We declined, especially after seeing the guy with knots all over his head! Mint had him straddled, so we pulled Mint off of him, because he seemed to be in a lot of pain. When Mr. Angel Dust got up, he ran like a thief, without looking back, and we never saw him again!

Lance was Mint's overweight kid brother. He always wanted to follow our crew around. If we played ball, he wanted to play. When we talked to girls, he managed to show up. He was like a Bae Bae's kid; you couldn't shake him, but what could we do? He was Mint's brother.

Wayne, a lover of basketball and Casino's younger brother, was my brother from another mother. Wayne was quiet and stayed out of trouble. He was the kind of person who always tried to do the right thing. Wayne and Lance seemed to get along well. They hung with our crew for a minute, wanting to be like us and trying to do the things we did, but we didn't let them hang around us all the time, because we were afraid that they might get hurt.

Casino was Wayne's older brother, who was definitely my brother from another mother. I would have probably died for this guy, because we were inseparable. Casino was a karate kicker, who was real quick with his hands and feet. He was free-spirited – a heart of a lion type of guy – but when he got upset, it seemed as if his head would spin around, and at that point, the devil was unleashed! He was the kind of guy whom you always wanted to be around. When he laughed, if you weren't there, you had really missed something funny. I always kept him laughing. When he rolled through the block, you could see him coming a mile away. His bike had multiple mirrors all around it and you could hear his bell-bottoms flapping in the wind as he rode. The ladies loved him and he could pull the best of them, because he was such a gentleman around them, but a beast amongst men. I didn't understand his methods until much later in life. One thing about Casino is that he took no sh.. from anybody. I was so afraid that someone was going to hurt or kill him, so I stayed close by his side. I was actually closer to him than my own blood brothers. If one of us had a problem, we felt indebted to the other to intervene. I remember an incident that took place at a roller skating rink, wherein he grabbed a guy and threw him on the floor. I don't remember what caused him to attack the guy. There was also another incident that took place while we played ball at Bellevue Hospital. This was my beef, because a guy came out of his face and him and I were about to fight. I heard Casino's voice and before I knew it, Casino had walked up to the guy, swung at him and laid him out! Then there was another incident at the bar on Sutphin Boulevard. Some guy pulled a gun out and Casino grabbed the guy and pushed him back. Casino left me with plenty of nightmares on what could have been my last day on earth.

My most memorable incident was at the club, Encore, with our friend Steve. This was our Thursday night spot, where we got to sit back and unwind. So, a friend of ours was dealing with a married woman, and her babies' father wasn't having it. I don't know how he found out, but he was plenty upset. He and his cousin showed up at the club and they saw Steve outside and he was a bit tipsy. We heard over the loudspeaker that there was a fight outside. Since we didn't see Steve, we ran outside and saw a crowd watching the fight go down. We realized that it was Steve and the other cat, Ed, on the ground in the middle of the street, swinging at each other. We intervened and managed to break them apart, but not before allowing Steve to get in a few more punches. He was our boy, and that's what boys do!

The next night, while chilling on the block, Ed and his cousin, Cas came walking along. Cas had on a white suit, and looked as if he was just coming from a wedding or something. He had his hands in his pockets, as usual, but we knew something was up, because he didn't say a word. All of a sudden, Cas pulled out a gun and started waving it! Before we knew it, Casino grabbed Cas, picked him up and threw him on the hood of a car. I felt that my brother had ESP, because it seemed like he knew who was going to shoot and who wasn't. Why else would you grab a guy holding a gun in his hand, unless you had a death wish? My mind wouldn't let me believe that, but nevertheless, we could have died that day! Casino, if you get a chance to read this, know that life had to pull us from each other, because the power that we had together would have killed one of us. One love for life my brother!

The last one to make up my team was yours truly. I consider myself to be a cool, calm and collective type of guy, who smiles a lot, has a healthy appetite for working out, and at that young age, was invincible. My jailhouse fighting skills were incredible and my martial arts feet were outstanding. Most guys were intimidated by my muscular build. I could jump gates as high as 7 feet, using just my arms. My luck was so good; it was as if someone was always there looking out for me and whispering in my ear. However, when I was angered, there was no telling what I would do. I might have tried to run through a brick wall or rip the roof out of a car or something; at least that's how I felt.

The most interesting thing was that when I talked, the guys got quiet, because they wanted to hear what I was saying. I was the voice of reason. I always listened to them talk about their problems, ideas and thoughts. I guess I listened to them to figure them out. Yeah, I was more of an analyst. I was free-spirited; if I liked you, you would know it, but if I didn't, you would know to stay away from me.

"Trouble" was an old friend of mine. He managed to find me at times, because I surely wasn't looking for him. I was one of the few guys who knew when to pull my hand back and walk away when the fire got too hot. Trouble found me one day as I stopped by a corner store. I was in the car drinking a Calvin Cooler, waiting for my partner to exit the store. I looked up and saw my partner being beaten up by two store owners, with his back against the glass. I rushed to his rescue. This was the first time that I had ever seen the inside of a jail cell, and it wasn't because of something I did. The store owner said my partner tried to rob the store, so he was being charged with armed robbery. I was eventually let go, because the storeowner told the police that I wasn't an accomplice. I was glad, because I was thrown in a cell with tight handcuffs on, along with four criminals. I had a look on my face as if to say, "Ya'll don't want none of this!" I could've probably beat them down, handcuffs and all.

I remember the time when I picked up one of my partner's, who lived on my block, to go and hang out. Without my prior knowledge, he had placed his gun underneath the passenger's seat of the car. This car had been driven by my family, mostly my mom, for the past week! A few days later, he called me to ask for the gun! I was livid, because he could have put my family in harm's way! The angels were truly watching over us during this time. I eventually gave it back to him – with a couple of choice words sprinkled in.

So, there you have it – the team. We weren't killers, but at any given time, we would have killed for each other. We had a bond, like the "Band of Brothers." Give a guy the backing of his friends and you will see just how powerful he is. He becomes a totally different person who is capable of anything. Now you know how it all started!

It had been a hot, sunny day, and the sun was just going down. The boys and I decided to walk a few blocks to see what was going down in the neighborhood. It was me, Casino, Mint and Willie Wilkins. We strolled down different blocks, girl watching, laughing and just having a good old boys' day. Then it happened! Some guy yelled out, "You, come here," as we were passing the block. Casino looked at me and I said, "What's up?" He replied, "Let's do this!" We turned around and went down the block. There were so many guys that they literally blocked the light from the street lamps. They surrounded us, asking us for money. This was when I found out that my brother Casino had a death wish. Casino yelled back saying, "I got money and you ain't getting it!" Although I thought we were going to die that day, I wasn't about to let Casino go down alone. I positioned myself behind the loud-mouthed leader, because if he was going to swing on my brother, I was going to take his head. The leader reached for Casino's pocket, but Casino knocked his hand away. The leader saw me standing behind him and said to his guys, "Watch this guy behind me!" When they saw that we were no chumps, one guy said to the leader, "They should join us." We had been looking to get into something more exciting anyway, so we agreed to team up with them. They set up the initiations. The corner of Sutphin and 157th Street is where we were to meet up just before dark. Then it started. We were wrestled to the ground. They allowed us to fold our arms as two guys held us down, with one ramming his elbow deeply into our chests multiple times. They took turns doing that. They were ramming so hard that it seems like they were trying to reach the cement below. We were able to take it, but we looked over and saw that Mint was hurting. Casino and I told them to let Mint up and we'd take the rest of his initiation. That's how we were – all for one and one for all. We all figured the days to follow would be more exciting, at least when we healed. We were stronger now, because there were more of us and we controlled the streets. We called ourselves "The Five," which stood for the 115 – the area in which we were from, although it extended throughout Queens!

Our team was continuously growing, block by block, and we became a large family. We brought our girls in, their brothers, family members and we started initiating our own friends. We even initiated our younger brothers and they became "The Young Five." We continued to grow and became great in number at a time when the "Seven Crowns", "Savage Skulls," "Black Skulls" and other gangs were dissipating. At that time, it seemed like everyone wanted to be a part of something. The Bricks, the slang name for the projects in Queens, had alliances of their own, and they were strong enough in their own environment, so we respected that. However, South Jamaica, Queens, was being run by "The Five," under the radar of the New York Police Department (NYPD). Back in those days, there weren't many police harassments, and no one was targeting us, because we didn't sell products or carry guns. We let our fists do the talking, so it was just fist-to-fist beat-downs. With those kind of beat-downs, you at least lived to see another day!

The chant was "Power to The Five. Whenever we saw a fellow brother or sister, that is what we would say. This was also how you knew that they were down. Unlike gangs of today, we didn't use hand signals or handshakes; it was a simple yell, "Power to The Five," "Power to "The Five!" You would hear that call about three to five times per day throughout the streets. That statement meant that we were family. If you had a problem with someone and we walked by and you said, "Power to "The Five," we had your back, and it was no longer an individual problem. This was a beautiful thing in the 80's.

"The Five" could have also been known as a social group, due to all of the get-togethers and events that we had. When night fell, the freaks came out and most of us couldn't wait to see our comrades. Our day tasks were finished and we were ready for that nightlife! Mind you, most of the time it was just to stand around laughing, talking and to see who was doing what. It was all good, because we were together and that's all that mattered. We were very protective against outsiders. They would have to know someone within our team before we could trust them, and even then, we still watched them, because they posed a threat to everything. Believe it or not, all we had was each other, along with the mindset to protect the family. We enjoyed walking the streets in a group, seeing our fellow brothers across the street yelling, "Power to The Five!" We didn't drink, smoke and said no to drugs! We exercised daily to keep our bodies tight and ready for anything - and boy could we fight! We felt that we were invincible at that age! We were gods!

The problem with being part of "The Five" was that I was staying out until the wee hours of the morning, and mom and pop wasn't going for that! All of our parents tried to keep us off the streets, but we were a family. We knew that we had to go to school, work, and do our everyday tasks, but the streets kept calling out to us. We knew how bad the streets were, but we were "The Five" and we were fearless! With all of the scoldings, whippings, and telling us bad things about the streets, little did they know that my extended family was in one way or another involved in what was going on out there.

I remember coming home late one night, and my mom told me that if I came in late again, she would lock me out! I told her that I understood. I wanted my family to be safe, but I also felt that my extended street family needed me as well, so I decided to go against mom's warning not to hang out late. The streets had a real hold on me! So, that night, I came in after 3:00 a.m., walked up to my front door, turned the knob, and found that it was locked. I didn't panic though, because my street sense kicked in. I walked around the house to find another way to get in, and was quiet about it, so as not to awaken the people who were living downstairs. I saw a pipe that I figured I could probably reach if I got onto the windowsill. I caught hold of it, pulled myself up and onto the slanted roof, and entered the house through the kitchen window. The next day, when mom found out what I had done, she again warned me to stop hanging out so late. She found out that I had climbed through the kitchen window to get into the house, so she said, "From now on, I'm locking my windows and I hope you can find your way back down the side of the house! All you have to do is come in earlier, through the front door!" I agreed and had all intentions of doing so, but once I hit the streets, I would lose all track of time.

So, once again I was out having so much fun, and before I realized it, the sun was coming up! I knew that this was bad, because it was daybreak and this was definitely going to be a problem. When I went home, I didn't bother trying the front door, because I knew that it would be locked, so I went straight to the second floor roof. It was easy for me to get up there now. I tried every window, but they were all locked. All of a sudden, I saw my mom looking at me through the window. She said, "I told you so!" I looked up to the third floor roof and could tell that those windows were unlocked. Here I was once again, about to climb up on a roof that was a little more slippery, due to the apple tree that hung over it into the yard. I got up there safely and carefully made it to the window and hoisted myself in.

The next day was a holiday, so we slept late. When I got up, after my meal, mom came into the kitchen. I got up to put my dish in the sink and she said, "Sit here for a minute. I need to talk to you." I sat down, but was afraid that this would end with me having a sore behind. Mom continued, "Son, I know you love being in the street, and it causes you to hang out all hours of the night, so late until you are now coming in through the third floor window. That's pretty high! One day, you are going to slide off that roof and we won't find you until the next day! You may or may not live! I'm just trying to keep you safe!" I could see the pain in my mom's eyes and her fear of losing me, and I didn't like what I saw. I didn't want her to be hurting like this either. I pictured myself falling off the roof with no one around, so guess what, that was the end of coming in late for me. I told my street family that I had to be in the house by 11:00 p.m. They all understood where I was coming from, because they had been neglecting things at home as well. So it all worked out. I got to keep my street family all while being obedient to my mom. She wasn't asking me to stop hanging out with my friends, she just wanted me to be in the house at a decent time.

One of the main focal points of our getting together was basketball. We played ball on a daily basis. You should have seen the guys in the park. There were so many of us. If you weren't from around the way and you caused a problem, there would be no way for you to get out of the park in one piece. Yeah, there were those tough guys who brought their teams, but with only one way out of the park, even they had to be humble. Like they say, "A rat with one hole is fucked!"

SHADY FRIENDS

One of the greatest things a man can do for himself is to learn to drive, because you can situate yourself and maneuver through life much better by this means of transportation. You then become obsessed with all types of cars and the colors that they come in. That's a beautiful thing. If you don't have a car and are fortunate enough to have a family member who will allow you to use theirs, that's a beautiful thing too. My mom and pop would allow me to borrow theirs, because they knew that I was responsible enough to drive safely. It was also so that I could give them a hand every once in a while, and that I did.

I am a dependable and safe driver, but I had to be mindful of the friends that I let ride in my vehicle, because they were sometimes careless. I'm saying that, because one day my mom allowed me to borrow her vehicle for some things I had to do. I knew a lot of guys and many of them weren't on the up and up. So, as I was driving down the boulevard one day, I saw a friend. I pulled over and he asked me where I was going. I told him that I was heading to the Avenue (Jamaica). He asked if he could get a ride and I told him to jump in. I stopped at the gas station first and then drove to the Avenue. When I got there, he thanked me, we shook hands, and he got out of the car. I didn't see nor hear from this friend for a good while.

A few weekends later, on a sunny afternoon, I received a call from that friend while I was napping. I answered the phone and he told me that he had left something in my mom's car the day I had dropped him off, and he wanted it. Bear in mind that my mom who is a staunch Christian, had been driving this car for the past couple of weeks on a regular basis – back and forth to work, to the market and to the fast food restaurant. I asked him what he was looking for and he said that I would see it under the seat. He asked me to meet him on the corner of 116th Avenue once I got it. Mom was home, so I ran upstairs and got her key. I opened the passenger door and looked under the seat and saw a 9mm that was fully loaded! I ran back into the house and yelled upstairs to my mom that I was going to the store and asked her if she needed anything. I drove to 116th Avenue and saw my friend. I told him to get into the car. He asked me if I had what he was looking for. I told him that it was still where he put it. I said a few choice words to him and told him that he didn't ever have to worry about getting into my car again! I told him that this is my mom's car and that her life was in jeopardy riding around for these past few weeks with that gun in her car! If she had been pulled over for whatever reason, she could have been arrested if that gun had been found! Just think about it, my mom could have gone to jail, just because I picked up a supposed friend, who knowingly left a weapon underneath the passenger's seat in her car! This friend was a member of "The Five."

NO STRANGER TO VIOLENCE

In my youth, I was no stranger to violence. This goes back as far as public school. I remember when my friend Tony used to always bother this young lady, who I thought was the sweetest girl in the school. For no reason at all, he used to bump into her, pull her hair on occasion, and say things to her that weren't polite. I would often tell him to leave her alone, because she was one of the pearls in the school. He wouldn't listen to me, because he knew I liked her. He was right! She looked good, had a nice physique and spoke to everyone. Whenever she spoke to me, I would have a really nice weekend.

When graduation rolled around, Tony and I were in the band. He played the saxophone and I played the trumpet. That was a wonderful day for us; at least it started out that way. When the ceremony was about to end, we all lined up to walk towards the exit door of the auditorium. Tony was the first one in line and I was right behind him. The music was pumping and we were playing our instruments. As Tony went through the double doors, the young lady, who he was always teasing, was standing there with a knife about inches long. She stabbed him in the shoulder! I saw the blood as it streamed from his upper shoulder as she continued to stab him! It became a crime scene in the blink of an eye! The young lady was tossed to the floor, the knife was taken and the police were called. I knew that she was going to be arrested, due to the seriousness of the crime. I also knew that Tony regretted ever teasing her. I never saw Tony again after our graduation day.

Violence reared its ugly head again in junior high school. A friend of mine, who was a foe at first, got in trouble with several guys, one of which told him that after school on tomorrow, he was going to kill him by stabbing him up! My friend didn't really believe the guy. He asked me what I would do if it was me that had been threatened. I knew that my friend had a thick leather jacket, so I told him that I would wear that to protect myself. I remember watching old gang movies, where most of the guys wore leather jackets and fought with chains and knives occasionally.   They all wore those jackets as a means of protective gear. My friend thanked me for the information. I told him that he was brave, because most guys would've probably stayed home. He said, "If I stay home today, I'll be staying home for the rest of my life." We shook hands and walked down to the bus stop.

The next day, after school, we met up again and began walking from the school down to the bus stop together. I was glad to see that he was wearing his leather jacket. For some reason or other, there was so much commotion going on down by the bus stop, until we didn't even notice these guys sneaking up behind us. One of the guys pushed my friend. My friend noticed that this was the guy who had threatened his life. After he pushed him, he pulled out a knife. The guy's crew wouldn't allow anyone to intervene, so I couldn't help my friend out. He tried to stab my friend with the knife, right in his chest, but the blade wouldn't penetrate his leather jacket! The jacket had saved his life! Just then, the safety officers ran towards us and chased the intruders away from the school's ground. The safety officers took my friend back to the school and I believe they questioned him as to what had happened. When I saw my friend the next day, he approached me with a big hug to thank me for looking out for him. Later that evening, I received a call from his mother, also thanking me for telling him to wear his leather jacket. The intruders never came back to our school and my friend was later transferred to another school.

In the years to come, I managed to stay out of all types of trouble, with the exception of some occasional fights with neighbors, who thought that they were nice with the hands. I was a beast and they knew it. One day, a particular neighbor felt that since all of the women were around and watching, he would challenge me to a slap boxing match. We began the match and at one point, he started getting very serious and even managed to smack me once or twice. I had already smacked him so much until he felt that he had to get one or two smacks in. All of a sudden, I felt a hard punch, so I began punching him back! We were supposed to be slap boxing, but this had now turned into a real fight. I hit him in his eyes and they swelled up like a grapefruit. After someone broke up our battle, people were asking why I had hit him in the eyes, and I said that that's what he gets for trying to show off. For years, we had been boys, and he knew what I was capable of, so he shouldn't have started with me. We were so close that his mom called me to come over to her house to find out what had happened. I explained to her that her son started to show off and that I had to put him in his place. She always respected me and the way that I treated everyone, especially when it came down to her family. She also knew how her son was. That fight caused a serious falling out between the two of us.

The next day, when I went to the park, he was there. He approached me, along with his friends, and said, "Alright… you got that off, so let's go!" I told him that he needed to think about what he was doing, because this time around, I was really going to hurt him. That was the end of our friendship. Instead of reacting to what I said, he just walked away, and that was a good move on his part. Years later, we ran into each other and it was like water under the bridge. Sometime after that, I found out that he had passed away. Despite our spat, he was a close friend of mine.

PRODUCT OF THE STREETS

During my early school years, I would play ball before going to school in the morning, just to burn off some excess energy. It seems like my friends and I never got tired, so after school we would get together again to exert some extra energy, whether it be fighting or playing basketball. This is how it all started.

At an early age, I found myself always wanting to be in the streets, although mom and pop gave me everything that I needed. Although I had fun with my siblings, I wanted something more. This is when I started hanging out late at night. I knew mom and pop would be worried, but it was a fix that I just had to have. They tried everything to keep me in the house, but I just wouldn't stay. At first, I began hanging out until 1:00 a.m., but when I got more involved with the streets, I'd be out until 4:00, 5:00 or 6:00 in the morning. My parents constantly spoke to me about it, but I never seemed to understand, because the streets had such a hold on me. I knew that they wanted nothing but the best for me, but I just couldn't seem to let the streets go. I was called over to a friend's house one rainy night, because he said that his mom and pop were fighting. I put on my rain jacket and ran over to his house. As I approached his house, I could hear his parents arguing inside. I was nervous, but I jerked the door open just the same, so fast until the glass portion of the door burst. I was young, with no income, and I was frustrated over hearing them argue. I didn't know what I'd be walking into if I interfered, so I took off running out of fear. My friend was going to have to handle his parents alone. If they hadn't been fighting that night, I would've stayed. Even at an early age, I knew when to get out of the line of fire. I didn't react like others would have. I always thought outside of the box, and people knew that about me. Some loved my ideologies and others were envious of me.

When I was in intermediate school, I remember this big guy, who used to stare me down with that 'I can't stand you look.' It didn't matter who didn't like me; you just needed to stay away from me. I had friends who were about their business and were ready to fight. I also didn't care who was there or where we were; if you disrespected me, you were going to get it! So, on this particular day, in the back of the school, the big guy, who was twice the size of me, decided that he was going to start up with me, since I had knocked his glasses off before. He charged at me, picked me up and threw me down on the ground. I hit the ground hard and had bruises to prove it. When we returned to class, our teacher called me up and asked me what happened. I told her nothing happened, but the big guy told her that I had punched his glasses off and a fight ensued. Back then, instead of calling your parents, the teacher would place you in the back of the room and you had to extend your arms while she placed books on them. You would have to hold those books until she told you to put your arms down. If you couldn't hold your arms up, she would then call your parents. I guess this just made me stronger, because I was back there a whole lot! It seemed like my fellow classmates loved to try me, or loved to see what I would do in certain situations. On a separate occasion, I was dared by another classmate to rip up his report, so I ripped it up, and to the back of the classroom I went. As long as mom and pop never found out about this, I could repeat this behavior every day. So, what did I learn from this experience? I learned that everything you do has a consequence.

It occurred to me one day that I wasn't just an ordinary kid. Here's one prime example: One day, my neighbor's two sons and I got into an argument. They were surrounded by their family and were popping all types of stuff. I saw that there was no way for me to get to them at the time, so I had to find a way. I knew what time they left for school and I knew the route that they took. I decided to set my alarm clock an hour before they would be coming out of their house. I ran out of my house, along their route, and looked for somewhere to hide. I found some bushes and hid there. In about 20 minutes, I saw them walking towards me, laughing and talking, without a care in the world. As they approached the bushes, I jumped out and said, "What's up now? There's no family to protect you now!" I could tell that they were scared, because they didn't appear to have the same heart that they had when their family was around. They tried to continue walking, but I jumped in front of them every time. I decided to let them go, because I knew what they were all about. You see, the bitch comes out of a nigger who ain't about his business. We eventually became friends later on in life and all was forgotten. As I look back over my mind and reflect on that day, I say to myself, 'What kind of child sets an alarm to hide in the bushes to confront two known enemies?'

- CHAPTER 2 -

LIGHTS OUT BALDY

It was an extremely hot summer that year. The heat was unbearable in the house in the evenings, so families sat on their porches to catch a breeze. You could hear the echo of the drums being beaten in the projects and you could see the children having fun in the streets. It was a summer to remember.

We all knew that we had a 10:00 p.m. curfew, because there were so many gangs around back then, and it was very dangerous to walk the streets. Although mom and pop tried to keep us of the streets late at night, we had friends who were night crawlers, and we loved them because of the stories they told. Mind you, my siblings and I were children who grew up going to church every Sunday, because our mom wanted to make sure that we had the fear of God in us at an early age. She also put us in the choir to keep us active in the church and to make sure we stayed out of trouble. Out of her five kids, I guess she knew one of us would wind up in the streets; that one child was me. In order to be in the streets, you had to become streetwise. This is why I gravitated towards any energy from the streets.

In my earlier years, I was blessed to have a wonderful friend named Bernard, who went by the name of Baldy. He was a very cool, calm and collective guy, when he was around his family and friends, but got agitated when outsiders came into his space.

He was older than me, and he knew a whole lot. I wanted to
learn some of what he knew and he was eager to teach me, so we
started a close friendship.

You see, Baldy had been in prison and had learned the art
of boxing; this was part of his present training. So, the first thing
I wanted to learn from him was how to box; they called it "jail
housing." He was one of the greatest jailhouse boxers that I had
ever met. His hands were so quick, and the way he boxed was
unlike anything I had ever seen. I had seen him box guys, using
a special technique, and I had never seen that kind of fighting on
television, although I had watched many boxing matches with
my pop. I wanted to learn how to box like him. He told me that
since he had been in prison, he learned the skill of boxing and
would teach it to me.   He told me that I would have to
continuously practice to get good at it. He said that we would
box periodically, and he would let me know my progress. We
practiced in the backyard during the day, the evening and at
night, and I wound up getting really good! I couldn't help but
to get good training with Baldy! While teaching me the skill, he
also explained to me what prison life was all about. "A smart
man knows when to walk away, so only use what you've learned
if you can't talk your way out," Baldy would say. He knew that
I was anxious to get into the streets to test my skills and see who
could beat me.

Baldy and I became inseparable. Although he was a little
older than I was, it didn't matter, because I always wanted to
hang with him. Whenever it was time for us to roll, Baldy would
always yell upstairs to me, "Jr., let's go!" Wherever we were,
we always wanted the other one to know. We were sports
fanatics and played handball, basketball and stickball in the park.
Handball was our favorite though. He was a lefty and that left
hand was deadly! It seemed as if every time he hit the ball with
that hand, he would hit a killer. That wasn't the only reason we

loved handball. We loved it because women loved it also. The parks were filled with women on the handball courts and we would meet women of all races and from all over the place. Another favorite pastime of ours was to clean our Pro Keds together, scrubbing them with toothbrushes to get them sparkling clean, until he started getting a little money and began sending his to the cleaners. Baldy was a great guy to be around, because I learned so much from him, like how to think outside the box. He was the type of person who would see something coming and would be prepared to react.

At some point, he confided in me and told me that he was a gang member, and he wasn't too well liked by rival gang members. He was a member of the Seven Crowns, a gang that ruled parts of South Queens in the 70's. Their name spoke for itself. Everyone knew of the Seven Crowns and what they were capable of. The only time the Seven Crowns would have Baldy's back was when they were fighting; other than that, they didn't support him in any other area of his life. Since Baldy and I were so close, he would sit with me on the stoop for hours, telling me of the events in his life. He shared how he and his gang would beat people up using bottles, chains, bats and all types of weapons. We also talked about the girls we liked, and the chicken heads. He told me that he was involved with a rival gang member's girl. I thought that that was crazy, but at the same time, I was impressed that he had the guts to do that! Shit, I was young; what did I know about relationships anyway? I did know enough to tell him that he needed to watch himself though. Although I was several years younger than Baldy, he knew that I looked up to him and would have his back 24/7. At that young age, I only had half a brain anyway. If you dared me to do something back then, I would do it without hesitation, and think about it afterwards. Baldy knew that I was a great listener. He said many things to me that didn't make any sense, but I listened just the same. He knew that I would run across some of those same things in life one day and he was right! Unfortunately, my teachings from Baldy were very short-lived.

One day while I was home watching television, Baldy and my girlfriend rang my bell. They wanted me to go with them to the park to play handball. I wasn't able to go, because mom had laid out a list of chores for me that had to be done before I hit the streets, and I hadn't completed them. Baldy and my girl decided to go without me. A couple of hours later, there was a rather violent knock at my door. I could hear a female crying on the other side of it, but didn't know who it was. The knocks were so hard until I became very anxious and hurried to the door. When I opened the door, my girlfriend was standing there crying uncontrollably, to the point where she couldn't even get her words together. I brought her inside and managed to calm her down. I asked her what was wrong and she said, "They got him!" I said, "Who?" She replied, "Baldy"! I felt my heart leave my chest, as my legs got weak! I knew I had to help him, so I called our friend. Everyone was willing to roll to the park with me. My girl went home and I geared up for the worse. Just as I was proceeding down the stairs to leave my house, I heard a screeching yell, "Boy, where you think you going?" It was mom calling out to me. She grabbed my arm and continued, "You better not leave this house!" "But ma, they got Baldy," I said excitedly! She replied, "I know, and if you leave this house, they will get you too!" She jumped in front of me, blocking my way down the stairs. I knew that I was in for the night, because once pop got home, she was going to tell him, and he would give me the talk and watch me all night so that I wouldn't slip out...and that's exactly what happened. Later on that night, the phone rang so much until I had to take it off the hook. I struggled trying to sleep that night, because all I could think about was Baldy and what he must be going through! I was hoping that he was all right. I failed to mention that Badly lived downstairs from me, so we were just like brothers.

The next morning, when I came downstairs from my room in the attic, I saw the look on my mom's face. Before I could say a word, she said, "They killed him!" "No, No, No, No, No!" I shouted. I just couldn't understand this! How could he be gone? I knew that he could fight; he was the best! He taught me skills that have wowed people, even today. My best friend was now gone! I don't remember crying. I was really in shock. I just sat under the windowsill, hoping and praying that it wasn't true. I thought, 'Maybe he's on the run and they just got it wrong.' I later found out that my girl and Baldy were playing handball in the park and a rival gang noticed him. One guy placed a gun to Baldy's head and told him to come with them, so he did. They took him behind the supermarket and jumped him. I know that he must have fought back, because it was in his spirit to do so. The end result was that one of the guys shot him right between his eyes. He was found dead against the supermarket wall, in a sitting position.

His death didn't really hit me until I saw the hearse, with the limousine right behind it, pulling up in front of my door a few days later. As I peeked through the window, I knew that Baldy was gone for sure. What a sad week that was. One thing that popped into my head was that the Big Guy upstairs told mom to give me those chores on that particular day, and she also ensured that I wasn't going to leave the house on that day, because I would have been in the park with Baldy, and mom more than likely would have been burying a son! I THANK GOD FOR MY MOM! SHE LITERALLY SAVED MY LIFE THAT DAY!

Allow me to digress for a moment. In life, you learn about the boy who grew up with wolves, hunted with wolves and ate with wolves. All he knew was the way of the wolves. He gained power by being amongst the wolves. This power didn't come from being an individual wolf; it came from being a member of a pack – a pack that would kill for each one of his wolves. You then decide whether or not you want to become a wolf or get eaten by wolves. As I grew up, I learned that in the buildings (the Bricks) it was important to belong to a team. The only problem with that was having an extended family of team members, because when things went down in one family, we all had to react. I am now about to share some of the events that persuaded me to change my life.

WHAT'S IN A MAN?

It was a wonderful afternoon, so my girl and I figured that we would go to the park for a while. After some time at the park, we left and went to Burger King, since it was the closest eatery. Upon arriving at Burger King, we walked in and noticed a lot of frantic people. We looked to the left and saw a white security guard bleeding from three to four gunshot wounds. He was dead! It seemed that this security guard was trying to protect Burger King from being robbed. The problem was that he didn't have a weapon. I guess that the robbers felt the best way to deal with the security guard was to shoot him. It was a senseless murder.

It was a particularly hot morning, and after a long day of playing in the streets, we went to the park to party. The park was the place to be on that night with everybody feeling happy, laughing and grooving to the music that was playing. I saw my friend Tink. We hugged and began reminiscing about the good old times. Then came the bomb! Tink expressed to me that he had done some things in these streets that had made him a target. He had been ripping off drug dealers and distributors. "When you do dirt, you get dirt," Tink said, so he knew that it would just be a matter of time before they caught up with him. He said, "Thanks for everything. We had some great times together." He hugged me again and said, "Take care my brother," and then he walked away. A week later, gunfire erupted in front of the supermarket where Tink was sitting on a crate! Although the bullets struck him from every angle, he managed to stand up, fold his arms and then collapsed on the crate! Tink was dead! He had to do what he had to do to survive.

One evening, plans were made to hang out in Brick Town. It was supposed to be a fantastic evening for two young ladies, but one of them decided not to go. The other went anyway. The darkness of the hot summer night fell and the noise from the busy streets subsided. A house was being targeted for its supplies and hit men ran into the house and shot three people – two guys and one young lady. The young lady was shot multiple times in the head. We all knew this young lady from the block, and she was being looked after by her brother. Her brother was searching frantically for his sister. Someone told him where she was and he ran to that particular house. When he entered the house, he found Emergency Medical Service (EMS) at her side. She was pronounced dead and the sheet was pulled over her face. Her brother began to cry outrageously and he grabbed her arm and said, "Please move…do something so that they'll know you're still alive!" By the grace of God, he saw her move her finger! EMS saw it as well and rushed her to the hospital. She later recovered from her injuries and discovered that she was pregnant!

He was a quiet man, a gentle giant, weighing about 360 pounds. Food was his love. I had known him for years. He lived with his grandmother and took care of her. He would always be on the block, shooting the shit with the fellahs and having fun. I would see him in the local restaurant, and boy did he have a smile, but on this particular day, it would be the last smile that I ever saw from him. I believe that his heart gave out on him one morning, as he was on his way home, because they found him slumped over his car.

There was an auto mechanic who I used to bring my car to. He was an honest man and never tried to stiff me, although his prices were a bit high. One day, a man came into his shop complaining about his vehicle. His vehicle had been fixed by the same man who I trusted. The man was very upset, blurting out a few choice words, and then he ran out of the shop in a rage! The auto mechanic felt responsible for the mishap with this guy's car, so he figured that he'd refund his money. The money was rolled up in his hand when he walked out of the shop to find the upset customer. As he turned the corner, there was a loud noise – a shotgun blast! We ran to see what happened, and as we approached the corner, we saw the lifeless body of the auto mechanic lying on the ground, with his eyes open and a large smoking hole in his chest! The money was still rolled up in his hand. This was another senseless murder!

We all knew this beautiful young lady who was hanging around a crowd that was no good for her, but if given the chance, she would've been able to stand with the best of them. She played the night. She played the guys. She played the streets. The problem with playing the streets is that the streets have been around for a long time, so the game belongs to the streets. She apparently shat on someone and that was the wrong person for her to shit on! So, one day a jogger was passing the park and he noticed several black plastic bags that weren't in the garbage can. He became suspicious, because those bags seemed to be holding something more than garbage. Upon investigating, those bags held the chopped up body parts of that young lady! As the old saying goes, 'If you hang with dirt, you will get dust in your eyes.'

One rainy night, the prettiest, funniest little diva you had ever met, got dressed to go out. She stood about 5'4" and would always be calling my name on the block. She used to fight with her cousins, because she liked to be in control; that was just her personality. Since the weather was bad, she decided to take a cab. She let the cabbie know where she was headed and he proceeded to her destination. When she got there, she gave him his fare, got out of the cab and he pulled off, never looking behind. After driving about 10 blocks or so, he was flagged down by someone. He got out of the cab and saw that the jacket of the young lady, whom he had just dropped off, was stuck in the door and he had dragged her those 10 blocks to her death!

Playing ball was the popular thing to do back then. We would get home from school and then go straight to the park. We enjoyed the competition so much! There was this one guy who took the competition a step further, because he wanted to referee all of the time. He knew all of the rules for the game, so he became our official referee. The crowd was hot on this particular day and the games were very intense. There was no room for error! The referee made a call and someone there didn't agree with the call, so a baseball bat was swung, and the referee went down. He had refereed his last game.

Whenever we played ball in the park, there were times when we played on the same side and other times when we would play on opposing sides. When the game was over, we would show our love for each other with a handshake and a hug. That night, I saw him walking through the park, on his way home. He passed by some kids and noticed that they were playing around with a shotgun. He told them to leave it alone, because it was a dangerous thing for them to be playing with. As he reached the corner of his block, he heard a noise. He began running to his house. When he got there, his mom was in the kitchen. All of a sudden, his back began to burn and he mentioned it to his mom. She lifted up his shirt and saw several bullet holes in her son's back! "Son, you've been shot!" she yelled! He winded up dying in her arms.

Sometimes in life, you learn from your mistakes. You learn that the strong sometimes preys on the weak, and in return, the weak becomes strong. You learn that the have-nots will find a way to have. You also learn that every dog has his day. Most of all, you learn to get out of the way of devils, who consider the streets to be theirs. This is just common sense, because you hold no army larger than the police force or the military, and at any given time, you could be shut down!

"If a man can have only one kind of sense, let him have common sense. If he has that and uncommon sense too, he is not far from genius." - Henry Ward Beecher (1813-1887)

- CHAPTER 3 -

THE ACADEMY

The Academy was a wonderful thing. We ate well. We were up before dawn to exercise every day to ensure that our bodies were physically fit. We got to know the other ethnic groups pretty well, especially since most of us had never really interacted with other races on a team basis. We were now all united for a common cause – to fight crime.

I am the kind of guy who likes to befriend people to find out what makes them tick. It doesn't matter where you're from or who you are. I'm curious about other people's likes, their dislikes and what makes them who they are. I wound up becoming very popular in learning to perfect my craft, and uncover my magnificence.

We had a good time at the Academy and most of us enjoyed each other. The evening walks, the workouts and the classroom tests were funny at times. I remember a comrade by the name of Dean, who sat one desk up from me and one row over to my left. One day, we had a drug awareness class. I knew that Dean had a problem with syringes because he had confided in me concerning that. The instructor asked if there was anyone in the class who had a problem with syringes and needles.   He suggested that they step outside for this portion of the class. Dean just sat there.   The instructor pulled out the syringe, pointed it to the ceiling and I could see Dean cringing out of the corner of my eyes. All of a sudden, boom, he fell to the floor. Dean was out like a light! We rushed to his side and began fanning him. He soon came to, and boy did we have a good laugh! I think we laughed for the remainder of the day!

There were other events that also stood out in my mind. One particular one was when two white officers figured that they'd go home for the weekend to see what the power of the badge felt like. They soon found out, because I believe they both got arrested. When they returned that next morning, after our physical fitness training, we all lined up and faced the stage where the head lieutenant stood. He brought those two fellows up on the stage, gave a speech on what not to do, and literally ripped the patches from their sleeves. He then told us to about-face and turn our backs to those guys, because they had let the team down. I thought that this was a horrible sight, because to me, the punishment didn't fit the crime. It was actually a lesson for us all though - don't disrespect the badge!

Another instance that comes to mind was a tragic one with my fellow partner Greg. Two weeks before graduation, he went home for the weekend. He attended a party that Friday night, not knowing that it would take him to his grave. A fight broke out at that party and Greg tried to break it up. One teen pulled a gun and shot him in his arm and the bullet ricocheted to his heart. He died instantly! We all grieved at the funeral, giving our deepest condolences to the family. They thanked us for the wonderful times that Greg had shared with us. One very heartfelt thing about this funeral was that police agencies from near and far came to pay their respects. It was as if a Hollywood star had passed away. This was truly one of the saddest days that I had ever witnessed.

The Academy taught us to dislike inmates, no matter who they were, because they were considered the scum of the earth. We knew that we had to disregard some of that methodology, because we figured that we would eventually run into an inmate from our hood. The Academy also taught us to cuss, so if you had never spoken a word of profanity before, you would be speaking it here. I guess it was a form of conditioning on what was to come after you had received the job. The problem with cussing was that the white officers felt that they could freely use the word nigger, along with the cuss words, and that there would be no repercussions behind it. Boy were they wrong!

Before becoming a correctional officer, you had to pass a 6-week physical, mental and abilities test. It was a course designed to measure your agility, strengths, weaknesses and to discover just how much you care for your fellow man. The obstacle course was the one that the new jacks feared the most. If you didn't pass that portion of the training, it meant you were going home. This was a problem for quite a few of my comrades. You see, taking a test is one thing, but being physically fit for something is another thing. Most of the guys had never worked out a day in their lives. Imagine being outnumbered in prison and having to depend on them to have your back. They wouldn't even be able to run for help.

Well, after having run a couple of miles on a given morning, the group became less and less. Some people quit, because they either decided that the job wasn't for them, or that they weren't able to tolerate the harshness of the instructors. This was no problem for me, because I worked out regularly on a daily basis, so taking on the task at hand was going to be a breeze for me! I always looked for physical challenges, because I was an athlete in school. Some people just have that feeling of wanting to be the best at something; that was me. I felt that my physical agility was going to be my way in.

When training for the obstacle course, I had always been in the front of the line, because I was the best - the fastest. At one point, I decided to go to the back of the line to show the trainers that I wasn't selfish. Some of the other faster guys followed suit. It soon became a trend for the faster guys to drop back in line to help the weaker ones. This was a brilliant idea, because I noticed that no more guys were quitting. This gave me a lot of brownie points and popularity in the Academy.

For several days, we went to the gym to train and learn the obstacle course. I watched every small detail – from the clocks that the instructors wore on their necks, to how the instructors were conversing amongst each other. They ran these training events as if they were gambling rings, because they had their sections competing against each other to see which team was better. They would whisper a little something in your ear to pit you against the other guys. It seemed like they had this competitive spirit, because their name and company would more than likely be placed on a plaque somewhere. It didn't matter to me, because I knew I would pass the course. I am the type of person who sets my mind on a goal, and once I do that, there's no turning back; the goal has to be achieved. I just wanted to be number one. To ensure that I'd beat the previous record, every day after the meals, I would put in extra push-ups, extra workouts, and would stretch my legs. I would even work out before bed, because I knew that in order to be the best, I would have to do my best.

The day came for the practice run. We all met up at the gym and began stretching. I looked around, sized everyone up, and said to myself, 'This is my day to prove myself.' I watched as other runners ran their race and noted their time. I knew that I had to make every second count if I wanted to break the previous record. Just as I got up from stretching, the trainer came over to me and said, "It's your day." I knew he was right, because my mind, body and spirit felt as one. I knew that I wouldn't be beaten on this day. When it was my time to go to bat, I focused on running as fast as I could without making any errors. I listened for the whistle and I was off! My squad knew my skills and I had already told them that I was going to go all out! After my run was over, I saw the instructors getting together to converse. My instructor ran over to me and said, "You have a chance at the Academy record; you missed it by 3/10th's of a second." He asked if I thought I could break it. "Yes," I said. "No problem." I now had the formula: Pump the muscle until it stretches and this will give me the edge! In the obstacle course, there were stairs that had to be run. I thought to myself that if I were to jump the stairs instead of running down them, I would set a new Academy record! The whistle blew again and off I went! The funny thing is, I remembered the start of the race at the blow of the whistle, and the end of the race, but what went on in between, I had no recollection. All I remember is seeing my team standing up, clapping and yelling, while everyone around cheered! It happened! My idea worked! I had broken the record! It was 1986 and The New York State and Academy record was now mine! I ran my ass off and took my rightful place amongst the other record holders.

Now came the Academy graduation. I was asked to carry the U.S. flag to represent the New York State Department of Corrections and the Municipal Police Training Council. This was an honor given to those who were the best in each event. We marched in circles so that everyone could see us.   I had accomplished my goal, because as I mentioned much earlier, when I have a goal in mind, there's no turning back.

My reputation as a record holder had spread throughout different facilities before I had begun as an official corrections officer! I saw people pointing and heard their whispers saying, "He's the record holder." This meant that I was somebody, not just a regular Joe! To the white boys, I was God, and they wanted to know how I accomplished this great feat. One person said, "There were hundreds of officers that went through the Academy, and you managed to break the record. Tell me your secret." I replied, "Well, being black and growing up in a crime-ridden neighborhood, all you learn to do is steal televisions and run. You run from the cops, you run from your baby's mama's dad… you just run. Even in your sleep, you're still running, so I just pretended to be asleep." We all laughed. Then I explained to them that there are people who run fast, and there are people who can run as fast as they need to. I knew where I stood.

TRIGGER HAPPY

Most people say that the power of a man comes from the people that back him, as in church, for example. A pastor or priest has a congregation of followers and they cause him to have a lot of power. I say this, because when a weapon is put into a man's hands, he now has the power, because he has your life in his hands.

I can think of two events wherein I knew that my life was at stake. The first instance happened one evening, when my partner and I were driving home from work. We were on the Triborough Bridge and he was speeding. All of a sudden, two cops jumped out in front of the tollbooth and one of them reached for his weapon. When I saw him reach for his weapon, I reached for mine. He told us to get out of the car and put our hands on the hood. We complied. He saw our uniforms and asked where we were going. We told him that we were corrections officers coming from work. My partner told him that another car had just cut us off, and in order to avoid an accident, he had to speed up. The officer went for that story. He then turned to me and asked what was I about to do with my gun. He had apparently seen me reach for it. I told him that when he reached for his gun, I felt that he was going to shoot through the windshield, and the shot would've more than likely killed me, so I was ready to shoot first. "Jesus Christ, is that the way you think?" he yelled. "Yes, because I have a family at home just like you," I replied. He looked at me, shook his head and said, "You guys can go, but take it easy."

The other incident took place one Saturday afternoon. A friend and I figured we'd do some target practice, on State grounds, up in the woods, so we geared up a .357, a .38 and two 9mm's. We also had M80's and bottles that we used for target practice. The M80's were set in the trees and we took turns firing at them. The loud noise it made was amazing, but since we were deep into the woods, no one could hear us. We even took shots across the Hudson River to see whose weapon went the farthest. The fun we had was unbelievable. A good amount of time passed by, and then we saw a car creeping close to us. It was a white car with a green emblem on it, but we couldn't make it out. It looked like a Conservation vehicle, but we couldn't tell, because the driver was coming directly at us. We saw his hands and knew that he was white. He saw two black guys in the woods, with a number of weapons, so as he opened his car door, I saw him unlatch his weapon. I felt threatened, so I pulled my 9mm from my waist. I believe that he was so frightened until he didn't even notice the badges around our necks, although they were very visible. I knew one thing for sure, that I was going to be the one going home to my family today! We identified ourselves as corrections officers and he eased up and told us to put the guns away. He told us to go further into the woods, because, unbeknownst to us, noises had been heard and that's why he came to check it out. This was just a misunderstanding on his part. We had the right to be there, on State grounds, practicing as State officers.

The thing is, where I came from, trust had to be earned, especially when it came down to life and death situations. Did I trust him? No! Was my life in danger? Probably …especially judging from what is happening to people of color today. Let me get this straight: You shoot me and then you go home to your family and have a nice meal! I don't THINK SO!

DOWNSTATE CORRECTIONAL FACILITY

When you graduate from the Academy, you get tossed around wherever you are needed. It just so happened that I was needed in North County, as some call it. Downstate Correctional Facility is where I ended up; this was a processing center. All criminals who had to do state time had to be processed, and Downstate is where their information was entered into the New York State Prison computer. I knew that I had been placed on a long list to be transferred to Sing Sing, which was closer to home, but I had to stay there until my transfer came through, so in the interim, I made the best of it.

On the day that I had to report to Downstate, I was feeling a bit anxious on the drive there. I had never actually seen this facility before, and thoughts of what I'd be getting into flooded my mind. It took two hours from Queens to get there! I knew I would have to find a better way, but this would have to do for now. As I pulled up to the facility, there was a rather large welcoming wall. The officers parked their vehicles beyond that wall. As I entered the facility along with other officers, we all headed upstairs for the roll call. We stood in two lines, looking real sharp in our uniforms. The captain briefed us on all of the situations that were taking place in the prison; we all saluted him, and then parted to different hallways. Some of the officers paired up with each other, because they knew where their posts were going to be. Others asked questions, because they knew nothing about the facility. There was a certain area where all officers had to enter; they called it "The Trap". In that area, there was an officer who controlled two rather thick glass doors. He would open the first door, close it, and then look around before opening the second door. This was like seeing a movie to me. From that point forward, the facility branched out like that of tree limbs. At the end of each tree limb was a housing unit. As you walked up the stairs, you were buzzed into a glass metal door, and right before that glass metal door was a glass and metal bubble, where an officer would be stationed in the Control room. I entered the Control room and saw that the bubble had two secure locked doors on each side. 'Wow', I thought to myself; this was some space, shit! When I looked up, there were two rows of doors, one on the lower level and one on the second level. The doors were positioned where the officer had clear visibility of each one. The controls in that room opened all of the doors simultaneously. If the officer wanted to let a particular inmate out, he would have to go to that cell with a key and unlock it. What a system!

Like all reception prisons, the Sally port is the area where new inmates come in, get cleaned up, and get checked for contraband. All body cavities are checked, their hair is cut off, and they have to wash their bodies with soap that is used for horses. Every officer has a task: one takes care of the bullpen, where the inmates sit awaiting their services, another does the paperwork, one is in charge of the haircuts and another monitors the showers.

I made myself at home in Downstate. The only hard thing about this job was staying awake for those 8 hours. An hour to hour radio check would be done throughout the night and judging from the voices of the other officers on the radio, everyone was asleep. 'Yeah, this would be an easy retirement,' I thought to myself.

- CHAPTER 4 -

FIRST SMELL OF A PRISON

I finally received my transfer to Sing Sing! I was happy about the fact that I would no longer have a two-hour drive to work; it would now be 45 minutes! Sing Sing was a maximum-security prison known for its fame and notoriety. This prison has housed the best of them, from David Berkowitz (Son of Sam) – a serial killer who shot 8 people , Jeffrey Dahmer – a serial killer known for dismembering, cannibalizing, lobotomizing and sex with corps. Willie Sutton – a 40 year bank robber, Albert Fish, who decapitated a 10 year old girl, and Ruth Brown Snyder, who murdered her husband. Those were just some of the violent criminals, some of whom are awaiting the death penalty in Sing Sing's Hot Chair, which was every man's nightmare. When you're in that chair, sometimes the electrical charge doesn't go off right away, but you shouldn't expect to be let go, because they will try it again, and even the Constitution can't stop this process from going forth a second time. The Electric Chair was otherwise known as "The Yellow Mama," "Gruesome Gertie", "Sizzling Sal," or "The Hot Seat." The execution itself was referred to as "Riding the Lightening". My personal favorite was "Old Sparky," because it entailed a bit of humor.

For criminals who are going to the Electric Chair, the night before, you're allowed to have the meal of your choice. It didn't matter what it was, they would get it for you, with the exception of alcohol; I guess they wanted you to feel the pain. This was known as your last meal, and it truly was. Old Sparky wasn't for everyone though, just for those who had no business being amongst civilized people, because they had no regard for human life. Those individuals would be put in a cage for a number of years, and more time would be given according to the severity of the crime. In other words, a person was given 15 years or so in the cage to teach him a lesson in regards to the crime he committed, but if he had decapitated someone, the time couldn't match the crime, so Old Sparky would be waiting for him. The Electric Chair sits in a room, just as lonely as hell, waiting for that door to open, waiting to be charged up. When it's fully charged, you're talking anywhere from 2,000 to 2,200 volts of electricity! Damn, that's a Hot Seat for real! Those criminals that I aforementioned already knew about Old Sparky. You see, there's a difference between a professional criminal and an amateur one. The professional criminal knows the consequences. He knows if he robs a bank and gets a certain amount of money, he'll bury it, do his 10 to 15 years, and when he's released, he'll be set for life. The amateur criminal will rob anyone without having a real plan in place, go to jail, continue to rob his fellow inmates and wind up dead. I've seen it happen.

The point I'm trying to make is that I knew a lot of criminals, and I've seen television shows about some; so what would make me do what I did, knowing that someone could've gotten killed and that Old Sparky might have been my Hot Seat?

Was it that I was an amateur, not thinking of the consequences, or did I believe that I could gain some sort of prestige without any consequences? Every action in life has a consequence, and I had yet to learn otherwise. If you have any thoughts of being a tough guy, think again, because you may not like where it lands you! It just so happens that I was lucky!

THE APPROACH

I drove anxiously down the block to the prison, not knowing what to expect. Sing Sing, which resembled a castle, was surrounded by a body of water, and appeared to be in a separate part of the world. I would soon find out that all of the horror movies that I had ever watched, had depicted prison correctly. There was a wall that stood about 40 feet high in the air, with armed correctional officers in the towers; they were the lookouts. I was truly grateful to be going to Sing Sing as an employee and not a permanent resident! I pulled into an open gate, which was on the outer skirts of the building, and parked. I was excited, yet nervous, so I sat in the car for a few minutes, just gazing at my surroundings, because I had never seen anything like this before. When I got out of the car, a guard in the tower pointed me in the direction that I should walk. I was now heading further downhill. I turned into what had to be the main building, and to the left of that building was an arsenal. I saw officers retrieving their guns from the arsenal as they were on their way out of the facility. Weapons also had to be turned in when entering the facility. We all had guns up in that piece! I walked towards two giant wooden doors that opened automatically. There was a metal detector and an officer, who was sitting at a desk, beyond those wooden doors. The officer appeared to be watching everyone very closely. All of us new officers were briefed and received our assignments from an officer known as The Watch Commander. We were then handed keys and we proceeded to our designated assignments. Some of us were assigned to relieve officers who were in galleries; others teamed up with officers as a sidekick. I had never seen so many serious faces in my life, all clad in blue uniforms. The inmates, who were clad in green, were serious too, letting us know that this was their home. My fellow correctional officers seemed to enjoy the code of the officer – dark blue pants, light blue shirt, black belt and black shoes. Whenever there was a problem and we saw blue outfits, we knew that help was on the way.

The officer who I had to shadow was very serious. I guess he wanted to prove to me that he knew his job and that he was going to give me a good example of how it should be done. (The thing is this, if you've been in the streets, you have a good sense of whose fronting and who is real, because it will show on their faces, and I was really good at deciphering between the two.) I was also able to tell who was a racist and who would have my back. I was able to decipher all of this on the first day, so in two weeks' time, I would be way ahead of the game.

I was a quick learner, so it didn't take long for me to get familiar with the facility as the officer showed me around. He was extremely talkative and I just wanted him to shut his mouth for a minute so that I could take in all that I was seeing. Although he had all of that mouth, my instincts told me that if a problem were to go down, I wouldn't be able to depend on him to back me up. We reached a gated door and he yelled inside and said, "On the gate". I heard the jingling of keys and soon saw an officer walking towards us. He opened the gate and swiftly locked it behind us. I was a little surprised that no "Welcome" came from this officer. I could hear multiple people talking, but didn't know where it was coming from until I looked up and saw nothing but gates and cells. This housing unit was of several tiers. 'Wow', I said to myself. I had never seen anything like this before!

The Control Office was referred to as the OIC, and on the back side of it was a housing unit, which was basically controlled by the inmates. There were telephones, televisions, and picnic benches all around. This was a whole new world for me. There were multiple inmates, a lot of movement, and three exits – one on each far corner, and two of them were always locked with a key and chain. The other exit, which was in the center, was only to be opened for changes in shifts. 'So, let me see,' I said to myself; 'If a riot were to break out, I couldn't exit through the center gate, because that couldn't be opened. If it was just a white officer and myself in this area, what would I do? Would I start swinging and keep swinging until help arrives, or would I just stick my head between my legs and kiss my black ass good-bye?' I preferred to do the first one, because I knew what I was getting into when I signed up for this shit!

SING SING CORRECTIONAL FACILITY

Being at Sing Sing was so surreal and exciting to me, because I just couldn't believe that I was walking and talking with notorious criminals on a daily basis. Some officers start out being nervous about what has to be done, realizing that one small error could cost them their life. That wasn't a real worry of mine though. My workday began at 7:00 a.m., along with 1,000 plus other staffers. We had the task of maintaining custody care and control of a population of 1,700 inmates until 3:00 p.m. For the most part, my days went pretty well and I got along with all of the officers, even the ones who didn't seem to care too much for me. In time, they learned to know who I was and what I stood for. I was cool, calm, collected and didn't mind dealing with problematic situations, because I knew how to handle them. We would basically adhere to the wants of the inmates, whether it be an officer complaint, grievances, medical attention, vocational programs, religious services, drug and alcohol treatment programs, counseling services or recreational needs. The routines were the same, but each day was different, because there was always something going on. The officers would often bad mouth each other. They would discuss their paychecks and how their ex-wives were getting all of their money for child support. They discussed what they had purchased, who they were screwing and how skilled they were with their guns. The inmates had simple conversations like discussing their privileges, their families, what they were going to do when they got out, and some of what they had done to be imprisoned. They didn't talk much about each other.

Being a rookie was tough, because the inmates would try you. I guess everyone received the same treatment at first. It was a means to see just where you stood. Although I smiled a lot, people knew where I stood, but they still wondered what was behind my smile. It was simple: If I smiled every day, you'd figure that I was a calm, passive person, but if I came in one day upset or looking troubled, that would show a different side of me, and you wouldn't know what I was capable of; I chose to keep it that way.

Each new day at Sing Sing presented something new and exciting, whether it was an officer challenging an inmate or an inmate boasting about how bad he was. I remember the day when we were in training and were taken to a State Prison named Greenhaven, where we had to stand in the cafeteria as a group, while the inmates looked on. If you had never been introduced to a prison environment, this type of situation would have made you shit on yourself, because you'd be thinking that your life was about to be taken by the lowest of the lows. I could tell that those were the thoughts of the white officers, by the beads of sweat that were pouring down the sides of their faces. They couldn't wait to graduate so that they could fully assume their power. As the days and weeks passed by, the routines got easier. Most of the black inmates seemed to feel a connection with the black officers. I could tell, because they would strike up a conversation about something or try to find things out about you. That wasn't a real problem for me, because we basically came from the same streets and if they wanted to find out about me, it would have been easy for them to do. There are thousands of inmates in prison facilities, and they have passed through many neighborhoods, perhaps yours as well as mine. People in general wind up knowing a mutual friend through a friend, so the world isn't as big as you think it is. There were a few white officers who were curious as to what the inmates did to get locked up. Some of them really wanted to understand the ways of the black inmates, but they didn't know how to get through to them and were unsure of how to treat them. Then there were other white officers who feared the locking of the gate, and didn't want to understand anything about the black inmates. They just wanted to collect a paycheck, carry a gun and a badge, and make it home safely to their families in the suburbs. Those officers were the ones that the system desired, mainly because they were focused on security and security alone. They didn't give two hoots about the inmates and did everything by the book. If the book said to give an inmate one roll of toilet tissue, that inmate would get one roll of toilet tissue. If the book said give an inmate one dessert, that inmate would get one dessert.

CAR POOLING

Three of my fellow officers, Bree, Frost and Man, discovered that we lived in close proximity to each other, so we decided to car pool to save on gas. This caused our ride to work to go by very quickly, because we were in good company. We would choose a particular day for one of us to do the driving, and that person would pick up the other three, for the 45 minute to an hour drive to Sing Sing. We wound up developing a great bond. We learned the likes and dislikes of one another through our conversations and the great music, which played for the duration of our ride. Bree was a Baby Face fan, and back then, everyone sang Baby Face songs, so we'd be riding and grooving along to the sounds of Baby Face. We actually became a team, never going against each other in the blocks.   This was considered a double code. We already had the officers' code, and now we had a code from a group of guys who were from the same area. The code was thick too. Let me explain: We had each other's backs, whether we were right, or whether we were wrong. Frost was the most troublesome one out of the bunch. I didn't know if it was his looks or his personality that made him a target, but guys wouldn't stop picking on him. Bree was a slim, strong-minded guy, who I trusted with my life. He would pass me often in the halls and would always check to see if I was good. We would give each other a nod to signify that all was well. The two of us had a special bond – a triple code, I would say. Then there was Man, a slightly older guy, who didn't want any problems, and always got straight to the point, so that he wouldn't have any. He was the neutralizer out of the four of us, because he always made a point of squashing any beefs. His character was very beneficial to us, because it kept us out of a lot of fights and from being suspended. It seems like we were always having problems with different groups of officers. The inmates had their conflict groups and we had ours. The blacks were with the blacks, the whites were with the whites and the Hispanics were with the Hispanics. We really didn't trust the Hispanics though, because they tried to work both sides – the Hispanics as well as the whites.

It had been a hectic day at work and most of us were beat. The four of us were walking down the hall and it was extremely noisy that day. I had a pounding headache. We were heading to the arsenal to extract our weapons before leaving for the day. I had just put my weapon into my pouch, and as we were walking to the car, Frost said something to me that caused me to flip. I grabbed him and threw him onto the car. Bree and Man grabbed me and pulled me off of him. They were wondering what was going on. I aforementioned that I didn't know why people liked to pick on Frost, but now I knew. He was about to get his ass whooped for what he said to me! On a normal basis, I always sat in the front with the driver, but due to my altercation with Frost, I sat in the back, to separate myself from him. Everything was okay for a while until Frost decided to open his mouth again and say something stupid. Bree said, "We pulled him off of your ass once; the next time you might not be so lucky!" Man said, "Frost, you need to shut the Fuck up!" He wouldn't stop, so I told Bree to pull the motherfucker over. I repeated it over and over. Bree wouldn't pull over, so I reached over and grabbed Frost by the throat, choking the sh.. out of him. Bree pulled the car over the shoulder of the highway and he and Man pried my arms from around his neck. Frost apparently wanted to see how far he could go before someone threatened his life. Well, he got what he wanted that day! I almost killed that nigga! As a result, the car pool came to an end.

- CHAPTER 5 -

KEEP LOCK REC YARD

The Keep Lock Rec Yard was the yard that contained gym equipment. There was a pull up bar, a dip bar and a couple of weights. Since it was located outside, the only comfort you had there was the heat from the sun, because there was no roof. When the small metal door of the Keep Lock Rec Yard flew open, all you saw was four brick walls, which were about 40 feet high; there were no windows and no other doors. There were two officers assigned to this detail. This yard was for the inmates who could not be in general population, because they were too dangerous to be around. They were fighters, stabbers, killers and they posed a threat to others as well as themselves. It is mandated by the State that these inmates must have an hour of recreation, so this was their space. On most occasions, there were no more than 15 or so inmates in this space. These inmates loved the Rec Yard and couldn't wait to get out there to let off some steam.

Most of the officers who had this detail came to this yard 15 minutes before the inmates got there, to get their own quick work out on. That's something that I definitely did. I would work out so much until I became a beast at it, with my pull-ups, push-ups, and dips. The inmates would be looking at me working out from the upper galleries and when they came into the Rec Yard, some of them wanted to compete with me, and I began competing with them as well. Working out was in my blood and it was great to be able to do it on the job.

I wasn't the only officer who was anxious to get to the Rec Yard; others were anxious as well. Some of them just wanted to see the competition, while others tried to bring back their youth by trying to compete, knowing that they hadn't worked out in years. The pride of man is something else! Some of them would rather wind up in the hospital than to say that they couldn't do something on a competitive level. Us officers were guys who worked together and even fought together, but outside of work, we had no time for each other, so that's why we made the best of it while at work. I always welcomed the other officers to my Keep Lock Rec Yard.

OFFICERS REC (GOTCHA)

The game of "Gotcha" was popular amongst the officers back in the 80's. This game consisted of catching you off guard, as real weapons were drawn on you, and then saying "Gotcha!" The game was taken from a movie in the early 80's, wherein the cast had to draw their guns faster than the other person. Upon doing so, they would say "Gotcha," and would win the game. We used to form pacts against other officers, wherein you'd be pulled over by a member of the other team, and his boy would produce his weapon and say "Gotcha!" We were a tight knit group of individuals who were just having fun, but we were having it with dangerous weapons. This game wasn't just played by correctional officers and state officers; the sheriff's department and city police used to participate as well. We had to be on point at all times, but there were times when we let our guard down.

One evening after work, we met in the parking lot. There were two teams of us, just hanging around, talking shit and having a crazy time. After a while, we got into the cars and pulled off. As we were driving down the parkway, we were pulled over by a vehicle with tinted windows. I was in the back of the car, so I slumped down in the seat and grabbed my loaded tech nine and covered it with my jacket, so that only the barrel was visible. A young man from the other car approached us and the driver began talking to him. Out of nowhere, his boy appeared and said, "Gotcha!" The driver said, "I don't think so; look behind me." When he saw the barrel of my gun, he said, "You got it." This was such a crazy game. We were men with guns, acting like children and having so much fun.

I'll never forget the evening when I was pulled over by a cop on my way home from work. I saw the flashing lights of a police car in my rear view mirror, so I pulled over to the shoulder of the road. A cop got out of his car, came to mine and pulled his gun out while saying, "Gotcha!" I didn't recognize the cop, but he said that we had a mutual friend and that our friend had just gotten out of his car a few blocks back, and he told him to follow me and pull me over. When he mentioned the friend's name, I knew just who he was referring to. I told him to let our friend know that he scared the shit out of me!

I remember another instance where we were being chased on the Sawmill Parkway by an unmarked police cruiser. We were weaving in and out of traffic, and I thought that the driver was an officer from the job. We were pulled over and to our surprise, it wasn't a "Gotcha" pull over! The driver expressed to the officer that he had no inclination that he was a policeman, because he didn't see any glaring lights. He told the cop that he thought he was playing the "Gotcha game. The officer understood and let us go.

There were two more memorable instances that took place after that. It happened a few days later when I was being followed by a county police car. The lights began flashing, so I pulled over. When the officer approached my car he said, "Gotcha!" Then again, within the next two weeks, I was awakened by the sound of loud knocks on my door. I looked out the window and saw a police car with its lights flashing. I opened the door and there stood two police officers with their guns drawn, saying "Gotcha!" As you can see, this was a hell of a game, because you never knew who was who with this game!

B-BLOCK ROVER

When you are given an assignment, you are to do that assignment until you bid for another one, or until someone's bid tour ends. The officers with the most seniority secure nice locations, such as working in the recreation area, the housing units, or being a transit officer. Those posts rarely became available, but when they did, they were open for other officers to bid on. If you were lucky, and no one else had bid on it, then you were awarded that position until you chose to leave it. There were positions that were considered power positions, and some of the smallest officers wanted to take them on. One position in particular is Officer In Charge (OIC). These officers are in charge of different Blocks within the housing unit – B-Block, A-Block, 5-Building, 7-Building, etc. So, with all of these Buildings and Blocks, these officers control the daily involvement of numerous inmates. The responsibility of these officers include: getting the inmates to their programs, to and from the cafeteria, to the medical unit to get their haircut, to school, to the movies, to the chapel, or even to work. The system was designed so that there would be a minimum amount of inmates moving at a given time.

A Rover's job entailed all of the above, so he had to be everywhere. He had to respond to every kind of situation in the Blocks, whether it be a fight, stabbing, hanging, wrist slashing, murder, or any other small incident. A Rover also had the responsibility of taking an inmate out to the Keep Lock Rec Yard. What a job! You get to see more than what the average officer does, but most officers don't want to see anything; they just want to do their eight hours and punch. That was probably best though, because this way, the officer would stay out of trouble. Officer Best and I were assigned to be the Rovers in B-Block, and we were all over the place! When an inmate decided that he would demolish his toilet seat with his bare feet, we were there. When someone threw bleach in the sergeant's eyes, we were there. When an inmate was hit in his head with a sack of weights, we were there. When an officer was getting his ass whipped on the upper gallery, we were there. When two inmates were fighting in the slop sink area, we were there. Yes, we would always be on hand to respond to these situations. We were Rovers, so we were expected to be there to assist or call for back up. Officer Best and I were a team, but I was favored amongst the inmates and Officer Best began noticing how the inmates were gravitating towards me. As they did so, he became less noticeable by them. He soon began acting like he didn't want to be bothered with me, because he was afraid of what I was becoming. He was slow to learn. More and more incidents were taking place and I could tell by the look on his face that he didn't approve of what was going down, but he didn't say anything.

The day came when my bid was over and I had to relinquish my position as Rover. Officer Best looked at me as if to say, 'Sorry my friend.' Our team as Rovers had ended. Another officer took my place alongside Officer Best, but was he going to have Officer Best's back like I always had? You see, everyone knew that Officer Best was my right hand man, so no one dared to mess with him, because if they did, they knew that they would have some serious problems with me.

One afternoon, I received a call that Officer Best was rushed to the hospital, due to a job-related injury. Some inmate had apparently taken a mop ringer and had swung it at Best. He tried to block it with his arm and it shattered his elbow. This left him handicapped and unable to perform the duties of a Rover, so he had to step down from that position. From that point, he no longer enjoyed his job, so he went out on ¾ pay. I heard that he was doing well, but this would have never happened if we were still a team.

WHAT'S IN A NAME?

We all encounter people with names that make you wonder how they got them, but there are some that speak for themselves, such as the name Madoff. Years ago, when you heard this name, it meant nothing, but today, it means a whole lot. Bernard Lawrence Madoff was a stockbroker, investment advisor, financier, and fraudster who ran a Ponzi scheme and basically cheated people out of their money for years. These people just looked right over the name Madoff. My point is this: wherever you go in life, you receive names on how you look, what you do, the things you've done and even the color of your skin. The Italians are famous for naming some of the mobsters, "Machine Gun Kelly, Mad Dog, Baby Face Nelson, Pretty Boy Floyd," etc.

I've come across the following names in my lifetime, and those names were very befitting of the reputation that certain people had:

"Homicide" got his name, because his crime was killing a person and stuffing their body in the trunk of his car, while going to the House of Pancakes. He got caught, because blood was noticed near the trunk of his car.

"The Iceman" got his name, because he was a murderer, amongst other things. I was fortunate enough to meet and talk with him on a daily basis, but I always noticed that there was something there whenever I looked into his eyes.

"Scar Face" was a stocky Hispanic guy who lived in a barbershop. His crimes were attempted murder and robbery. The scars on his face depicted that he was no saint.

The point I'm trying to make is that you don't just wake up one morning and decide that you want to be referred to by a certain name if you don't have the character to back it up. If you don't use wisdom nor know the meaning of the word, why call yourself wise. I have run across guys who have given themselves names that don't fit their personality at all. As Polonius in Hamlet said, "To thine own self be true."

There was an inmate who was known as "Big Jus" and he wore that name very well. He was called that, because he was a big, strong, stocky guy. He was a true dude too and many people admired him. Another inmate who wore his name well was "Shorty No Neck". He inherited that name, because his shoulders were so close to his neck. Shorty No Neck was not a killer; he was a street hustler with plenty of soldiers by his side.

THE WORKOUTS

It's in an officer's best interest to be physically fit in an environment where he is outnumbered and may have to run for his life, or better yet, come to the rescue of his fellow officer, who needs assistance in subduing an inmate(s). Do you remember Larry Davis? He was a cop's nightmare. When he was finally apprehended, he was brought to a state prison with bad legs, so he had to walk with a cane. One day, as he was walking through the hallway of the facility with a friend, an

inmate approached that friend and wanted to kill him. Davis
intervened and the inmate wound up killing Davis. My point is,
there were times when inmates tried to provoke us officers to
subdue other inmates who could care less about what happened
to them. If us officers got in the way of their conflict, we either
had to be physically strong or had to be present in numbers to
dissolve the matter. Most of the time, the officers were
outnumbered. It wasn't unusual to see an officer yelling or
running for help, because most of them weren't physically fit
and they thought it was just a job, especially the new jacks.
Those white boy new jacks mostly came from up North, places
where they didn't see black people too often. A white officer
once said, "Hey Brister! Where do you guys come from?" I
thought he was joking, but as the weeks followed, I found out
that he really didn't know a thing about the Black race. So
picture this: A white boy from West Bubblefuck is hired to treat
a brother fairly, firmly and be consistent with him, but he's never
dealt with Black people before. There's something awfully
wrong with that picture! I was assigned to work with these new
jacks for their On the Job Training (OJT), and I had to keep them
under my wing until their probationary period was over. What
a task that was! They were scared to death! I coached them and
told them to forget what they had learned at the Academy,
because everyone deserves to be treated as a human being here.
I told them that if they get assaulted, other inmates will look to
see how they respond to the attack. The black OJT officers
understood what I was saying, because they handled themselves
accordingly. The white officers were afraid to lose their jobs, so
when they got smacked around by the inmates, they would come
and tell me. I told them that I didn't want to hear it, because I

had already told them what to do in that situation. I guess growing up in different environments causes people to react differently. Lots of brothers were losing their jobs or were on suspension due to conflicts with inmates, but our environment teaches us that when you're struck, you must strike back, or else others will strike you too.

- CHAPTER 6 -

THE BEEFS

If you've had a couple of stripes on your shoulders, then you'd swear you were running things. I never had the stripes, but at one point, I was truly running things. You see, we were in charge of a large number of inmates with time ranging from five all the way to one hundred years of life. How could I, a plain old correctional officer, influence the best of the criminals? It was easy; find a common denominator, something that connected us as a people. So, I found it! It came in the form of competition. We all enjoyed competing, especially if you were incarcerated. So, as I received my regular post as the Keep Lock Rec Yard officer, I implemented my program, because that was a place where I would be isolated. The program was easy to implement, because it consisted of physical exercise. All we had in the yard was a pull up bar and a dip bar, so I planted the seed; I put the hook out there and waited for feedback. This stirred up the interest of the inmates who were working out, because instead of them staying in their cells for recreation, they would be competing with other inmates. Why wouldn't they want to come out to participate in something like this?

The program was designed right up under the nose of the

administration. I designed it to see which inmate was the fittest and that inmate would be rewarded accordingly. I ran this program for years, and it gave me power in the facility and respect in the Blocks. Whenever a fight, stabbing or attack on an officer was going down, I was probably one of the first to know. It got to the point where some inmates used to start fights just to be sent to the Rec Yard. The program was running so well that it caused me to be favored by the inmates, and they made it a point to protect me from other inmates and officers alike. If an inmate or officer said something about me, or was plotting anything against me, it would get back me. It seemed as if they wanted me to be around for a long time. I remember one particular inmate, who used to constantly give me problems in the Blocks. When I went to the Rec Yard, another inmate said, "You don't have to worry about him anymore, because in a few minutes you're going to hear that there's a fire in one of the cells, and an alarm will sound; that will be us handling our business, and it won't come back to you. That's when I knew that I had the power for sure!

There were numerous events that occurred that let me know I had the power. One day, an officer was getting beat down by an inmate on the upper tier. I had had a problem with this officer earlier that day, so the inmates decided to take care of it, and they did. I heard the officer yelling on the upper tier and we ran to his aid. Several officers were beating on one inmate. The inmate began grabbing at my leg, as if to say, 'Take me downstairs.' I interceded and took the inmate downstairs and locked him in the shower area. I asked him what happened. He said, "You know what this is about, and we ain't having it." All

I could do was shake my head. The power was there and it was all mine; I just had to control it. I decided to create teams, give them names and chose a leader for each team. Thus, the introduction to the Family and the Council was born.

The Family was a group of lifers who basically controlled certain Blocks. Within the Family was a lifer by the name of Iceman. He reigned in the mean streets of South Jamaica, Queens for years, and with this name, he needed no introduction. He controlled a large number of the inmates and believed in fairness for all. If an inmate was supposed to have something, he felt that he should get it, whether it be toilet tissue or a fair fight. Iceman and I were close and we thought alike; that is probably what brought us together.

The Council consisted of several officers who basically wanted peace and fairness in the Blocks. This desire was contrary to the desires of some of the other officers, who believed in the teachings of the Academy, wherein all inmates were considered garbage and scumbags. Only those officers with an open mind were able to eliminate that way of thinking. The Council's headman consisted of myself and another officer, whose name I'm not at liberty to mention. I do wish him well though.

The Family and the Council held regular meetings on what was going down at the facility. We met on the upper tiers and decided who was who – meaning that if an officer got out of hand to the point that the family couldn't stomach him anymore, they would ask if he was one of ours. If we said he was, that officer wouldn't be touched, but if we said he wasn't, then he would get whatever he had coming to him. There was mutual respect amongst the two groups. The Family provided the protection to ensure that the inmates received what they needed. No contraband was given, just fairness and other liberties. This was a wonderful thing, because there was a lot of cooperation between the inmates and the officers. As a result, the Blocks seemed to run a lot smoother with everyone knowing their positions. Whenever someone got out of line, it was brought to the table for discussion. There were those who wanted to handle certain situations themselves, and that was cool, just as long as they acknowledged the powers that be. We didn't care who you were or what team you belonged to – a sergeant, lieutenant- , lifer, chain snatcher, protective custody prisoner, or even the warden himself, if you got out of hand, you would've still gotten it. We had the power and the ability to squash any beef that arose in the facility.

The Family and the Council had a member from each team that had a beef with one another, and they wanted to settle it by fighting, so the head of the Family and I decided that it was time for them to do their thing. We would give them a fair one; a one-on-one in the Rec Yard. Like others before them, they knew what it was all about, because we had been doing this for years, and it had never been detected by the prison's administration. The prison's administration was run by a man who sat behind a desk, with bars on his shoulders, pants well creased and not a wrinkle in his shirt. He truly believed that he was controlling the prison from within the four walls of his office. How mistaken he was! He had sergeants, lieutenants, and snitches as well, but guess what, when they were in the Blocks with us, they belonged to us. We were the ones establishing the rules, not some man sitting behind a desk!

So, the fighting match was set up between an officer and an inmate. I didn't have a good feeling about this fight, because it would be the first time that I'd be allowing my fellow officer to fight an inmate. The officer knew what the rules were, so for him to even ask my permission for a one-on-one with this inmate meant that he either hated him or was just plain crazy. The process was simple: I would pat both of them down to ensure neither one had a weapon and the two of them would be locked in the Rec Yard so that no one could run out. The only view that I would have would be through the square window, which was approximately 4"X6", and I would have to block that window from the general population, so that they wouldn't be able to see what was going on.

A few days before the fight was to take place, I began itching uncontrollably all over my body – from my eyelids, to my feet, to my nuts! I went to the doctor and he said that it was probably stress, but he couldn't find anything to properly diagnose that. I figured that it would go away soon, and it eventually did. On the day of the fight, I woke up that morning saying to myself, 'This will be a day to remember.' My daily routine was the same: I came to the facility, checked my weapon in at the arsenal, and went through the main door. The sky was cloudy with a dark mist flowing over the prison. When I reached the Blocks, the inmates got real quiet. The only time it gets that quiet is when something is going down or about to go down. I saw all of the players in this event, and they looked at me as if they couldn't believe that I was going to allow this to happen. The officer who was involved, approached me and said, "Always straight." I replied, "Alright, today is your day, so make the best of it. Now you know it's going down." I took a walk up to the inmate's cell who was going to be fighting. I said, "You good?" He responded, "Yes." When you're in a prison environment, surrounded by many men, you are taught to be strong, and even if you are weak, you have to make it a point to show no signs of that weakness. This was the mindset that the officer was going with, but he wasn't thinking clearly about the consequences. The difference between a professional fighter and an amateur one is that the professional knows the consequences, but the amateur doesn't. If the officer had taken the time to think of the outcome, he would have never wanted to challenge the inmate, but this is what happens when men won't back down. My job was to set the fight up, and I did. I could tell by the look on the officer's face that he wanted to change his mind, but the reputation that he held would have been destroyed, because he would've never received respect from any inmate going forward. So, on that day of truth, there was no calling in sick or saying, "can we do this another day?" The stage was set and the fight had to take place on that day and if it didn't, the one who backed down would have been considered a pussy. Allow me to keep you in suspense for a moment while I digress a bit.

THE FAIR ONE (ONE ON ONE)

The "Fair One" was a privilege we granted to inmates or officers who understood the code. The code stipulated no talking about the Fair One, no fighting in the blocks, no stabbing in the blocks and waiting your turn to go one-on-one with your problem. Anything could go on in this yard, just as long as you had a lookout on the other side, and that person had the key. In order for you to get out, you had to knock for him to open the door. He would periodically check on you while he waited in the hall. Think about it though: You're in the Rec Yard with 10-12 inmates at a time, and if anything were to go down, and they really wanted you, it would be too late by the time help arrived. In other words, you were on your own! I had seen some white officers at this post and they didn't like it one bit, because they were scared to death of the inmates. I overheard one of the white officers saying that there was too much color in there. Wow! How prejudice is that?

One day, there was a problem on one of the tiers. Two inmates by the names of Slim and Yae were beefing, because they needed to get something off their chests. Slim jokingly said to me, "Can I use your yard to whip this nigger's ass?" I said, "No! You're kidding right?" He didn't answer and I walked away. When I returned to work the next day, I found out that Yae had almost stabbed Slim to death. This bothered me for weeks, because Slim was one of the inmates that I used to talk to when he had his down time or was locked in his cell. He would tell me what I needed to know and how to keep my people safe in the facility. Poor Slim never returned to Sing Sing. I heard that he was transferred to another prison after his recovery. Yae remained there, but stayed away from me, because he knew that I favored Slim. This got me to thinking that if I had let Slim and Yae knuckle up in the Rec Yard, Slim wouldn't have been stabbed. I was a young rookie though and didn't know any better at the time.

- CHAPTER 7 -

THE FIGHTS (DAY OF RECKONING)

JOHN VS. MORALES

John was a quiet guy, who I had seen in the streets, but had never really spoken to with nothing more than a little head nod, as if to say 'what's up or what's good?' It just so happened that he got caught up in a bad way and landed right in my prison. He was faced with a prison term of 10 years. When he saw me, it was some of the same old 'what's up' head nod. There is something to be said about where you're from or who you know in life, which causes people to want to associate themselves with you. I was from Queens and John was as well, so he felt a certain allegiance to me. If a person would say that they're from Brooklyn, or the Bricks (projects), it would be a means of association. So, if I were placed in an area of a prison, with nothing but guys from Brooklyn, and I was a first-time offender, from West Bubble Fuck, you better trust and believe that I would let those guys know who I knew in Brooklyn. They call that association, to keep the inmates off that ass. So anyway, on this particular day, an inmate by the name of Morales was acting unruly by yelling, running out of line, and acting as if he wanted to fight other inmates. He was also wearing a hat, which is forbidden to be worn in the halls. When we got to the door of the Rec Yard, I told him to pull his hat off, or else I'd be taking him back to his cell. He cursed me, but pulled it off just the same and ran into the yard. John sat back and watched the whole thing. He walked up to me about a half hour later and said, "Let me handle that for you." I said, "He's not a problem, he's just acting." John said, "You don't know what he's doing here. He's creating problems for a few of us in the Block. Now's the time to take care of this. All you have to do is make sure he's the last one on the line and shut the door before he can walk through." I began thinking to myself that it would be nice to get some payback. The bell rang and the recreational period was over. All the inmates grabbed their things and were lining up at the door. John and I stood by the door. As the inmates were leaving the Rec Yard, all of a sudden, Morales pushed the man who was in front of him and ran to the door, almost knocking us down. It was as if his sense of fear kicked in and he knew what was about to go down. John told me not to worry about it, because there were a couple of other officers who were looking to get him too, so he wouldn't get away with his actions. Morales never came back to the Rec Yard, and I heard that he was in the hospital.

SAM VS. PERRY

Sam was a tall, slinky guy, who was quiet, worked out a lot, and loved to play ball. He would sit back and watch all that went on; it was his way of staying out of shit. There were times though, when that shit just drew you in and there was nothing that you could do about it; you either had to pucker up or stand up and fight.

Well, on this particular day, in the Mess Hall, this slick, conniving, waste of a sperm guy, by the name of Perry, figured he'd pick on Sam. Since Sam was always quiet, I didn't know what he was capable of. I figured that Sam would either run away or snap, because every man that I've ever known since I was a kid had a breaking point. This was Sam's breaking point, because he snapped and we never saw it coming. He jumped on Perry and a fight ensued. It caused a huge problem for us officers, because there were only eight of us in there with approximately one hundred inmates, so we were out-numbered. We pulled the cord on our radios to signify that an officer was either in trouble or needed assistance, but wasn't sure how the responding officers would get to us, because in a riotous situation, the orders of the superiors are to lock the Mess Hall, so we were trapped like roaches in a motel. Whenever situations of this kind occur, each facility has a designated emergency response team in place to respond to the matter. They all go by different names, but they are all part of the emergency response team. Guy, who belonged to such a team in my facility, ran to gear up for the riotous situation. He and his team were a force to be reckoned with; each of them was flushed against the other's shoulder, wearing protective gear with a shield in front of them. All of a sudden, the door opened and someone on the mic yelled, "GET DOWN, GET DOWN!" All of the inmates hit the floor on their bellies with their hands on their head. The team then marched through the door and went straight to the problem. Sam and Perry were subdued and taken to the box – a place where they get some alone time. The amount of time that you stay in the box is determined by the lieutenant. It consists of a row of cells with a wall separating each cell. When officers go into that area, they normally have to push this fiberglass petition around in front of them so that they don't get hit with piss or worse. As Sam and Perry sat in the box, they yelled across the room to each other saying what they would have done if the fight hadn't been broken up, and what they were going to do when they got back in the Blocks. Soon after that, I was approached by some inmates (Perry's co-defendants) who asked me if I was going to give Perry a fair one in the Rec Yard when he got out of the box. I told them that I would see. I found it amazing that a fight could happen one minute and the next minute, a "kite" would be sent to me for a fair one to be set up. (A kite is a message sent from cell to cell to get to the individual it needed to get to.)

The day came when Perry was released from the box. That afternoon, I went by his cell and asked him what had happened. He said, "That bitch ass nigga was trying to extort me! I ain't having it!" I said, "His people approached me about a fair one. What do you think I should do?" "Set that shit up," said Perry, "He can't fuck with these hands!" He showed me his fists as he made that statement. So, I sent a kite to his people with the day and time for the fair one.

On the day of my normal security for the Rec Yard, and before the inmates were allowed to enter, I told my fellow officer to keep the hall post, because I was going to be in the yard and didn't want the door to be opened until I knocked. I entered the yard first and turned to the door. Sam was the third one to enter, followed by more guys and then Perry came bopping along like he was so big and tough. I patted both guys down, while the other inmates hit the wall. Sam put his hands up and Perry followed saying, "What's up nigga?" Punches began to fly and to the brick wall they went. Sam picked Perry up and threw him to the ground, kicking him in his face. Perry was done! I grabbed Sam and said, "He had enough." They both had brick marks on their skin from when they hit the bricks, but Perry had face knots and blood was coming from his mouth. They cleaned themselves up and chilled on opposite sides of the wall until the bell rang. When the bell rang, everyone formed a line and Sam and Perry were the two at the end of the line. I said to them, "Y'all know how this works, right?" They shook their heads and agreed to silence. Off to the gallery we went and the beef was squashed.

TREVOR VS. LANCE

Trevor was a yardman. What I mean by this is that he stayed in the yard on the weights. He was about 6'5" and respected me for some reason, but didn't care too much for authority. He would treat the white officers disrespectfully and they would let him get away with it. I guess they were afraid of him, due to his size and his attitude. He could be a piece of work some days, but he was about his business and inmates knew it. He was often with this guy Rich. Rich was on a skid bid for years and didn't want any problems, but if there was a problem involving Trevor, he was there one hundred percent; he had his back. Trevor had a beef with a guy named Lance. Lance was into something, because everywhere Lance went, there were at least eight guys following him. He was well protected and he had that walk that said, 'Fuck with me and you die.' He seemed to be one that the Blocks feared. I had been told that Trevor and

Lance kept eyeing each other and I knew what this would lead to, so I kept an eye on both of them.

One day, while I was on the main floor, chow was called. I was on the main floor and something caught my eye. Trevor, who was on the top tier, was coming down the narrow metal staircase with Rich, quickly. They were heading to chow, because they were kitchen workers. Lance and his crew were heading down the staircase as well. Trevor got through the downstairs gate, but when he turned around, Rich wasn't behind him. I couldn't see Rich either, due to how the staircase was constructed. Trevor yelled out "On the CO", so that he could run back up to see where Rich was. As soon as he got to the second level, he saw that Rich had been beaten up. Rich said, "They kicked my ass!" "Lance's crew?" said Trevor. "Yes!" said Rich. "Them fucking cowards!" Trevor helped Rich up and the two of them headed to the Mess Hall. I positioned myself in the Mess Hall where I would be able to see both sides – Lance and his crew and Trevor and Rich. Since Trevor and Rich served the food as kitchen workers, Lance and his crew had to get their food from them. I don't know about you, but if you're serving my food, that means that we're either the best of friends, or have a good relationship. Lance and his crew weren't that smart. The line was quite long. I watched as Lance and his crew got closer to being served. Then it happened! As Lance approached Trevor, Trevor snatched him right over the counter and started whaling on him. His crew was in shock. They tried to get over the counter, but the kitchen workers kept them back. I knew the cord on the radio had been pulled, because officers came from everywhere. Trevor and Lance were thrown to the floor and handcuffed. I walked around the crowd to see if I could get a view of Trevor's face, and I did. He turned, smiled at me and winked. He was headed to the box. I visited the box on a daily basis, so my going there wouldn't be something out of the ordinary. When I saw Trevor, we gave each other that 'What's up' nod, with no spoken words. He would always be doing extreme workouts on the floor, so I didn't want to disturb him with a whole lot of chatter. As I was doing the headcount on the upper gallery, I passed by Rich's cell and he asked about Trevor. I told him that Trevor was fine and was in workout mode. Rich said, "Lance ain't gonna' let this go." "I know, but don't worry; just stay low," I said.

Lunchtime rolled around for me, and as I was eating with my fellow officers, another officer approached me saying that the gallery port needed to see me. I went to see what this was all about and found that a kite had been sent for me to meet Ice upstairs for a talk. I knew that this kite would be coming sooner or later. I expected it. The Rec Yard call was made and I headed up to talk to Ice. We shook hands and proceeded to talk. He said, "You know that problem with Lance and his boys ain't gonna go away until someone is dead, right?" "I know," I replied. "We need to have a fair one to stop this! He said while nodding his head. "I got this Ice," I said. I then sent a kite to both inmates telling them that men fight like men, so hold all thoughts. This was the code for a fair one. They were still in the box, so they had two weeks to figure this out, before they would be released back to me for access in my Keep Lock Rec Yard. Again, this yard is for inmates who shouldn't be in regular population, due to fights or any unusual behaviors. Once they are deemed fit, they can be put back into regular population.

   The day came when Trevor and Lance were released from the box. The mirrors, which allowed the inmates to see what was happening down the halls, were all out. Both guys were double-locked in their cells; double-locked is when your cell is locked with a key, as well as by the officer's break in the middle of the gallery. So, everything was set up for noon in the Rec Yard. The plan was to pick up all of the keep locked inmates and take them to the yard. Before doing so, I approached Trevor and Lance to make sure they were still in agreement. Trevor said, "It's a go!" Lance started cursing and said, "I can't wait!" We picked up the inmates from the galleries. Trevor stood second in line, while Lance was with another officer in the rear of the line. I opened the door to the Rec Yard and the inmates proceeded in. Instead of them running to the equipment, they played the wall, because they knew what was about to go down. I handed the keys to the officer and told him not to open the door unless I knocked. Trevor got into a stand in front of Lance, looking like he was going to take Lance's head off. Lance said something and then he put his hands up. I didn't understand his fighting stance; perhaps he had never fought before. Then Trevor swung, hitting Lance in the jaw. Lance staggered and fell back to the wall. Trevor seemed to taunt him saying, "You ain't so bad without your crew!" I hated to agree, but Trevor was right. I have seen many tough guys in my days; some could fight without their crew, while others could fight without a weapon. Lance didn't have a weapon and he couldn't even knuckle up to fight. Trevor was beating him so bad that even I felt for Lance. I broke up the fight, because Lance had had enough! They cleaned themselves up. Lance was still running off at the mouth. I went over to Lance and said, "You do know what this was, right?" He said, "Yeah, but it won't change anything." I said, "If there are anymore problems with you and Trevor, many more will become involved and that won't be good." I extended my hand to shake his and he turned and walked inside. Trevor, who was waiting to talk to me, extended his hand and thanked me as he went inside. I had always heard the adage, "It's not the dog in the fight, it's the fight in the dog." That adage became perfectly clear on that day!

DINO VS. STRETCH

Stretch was a well-known shop worker who loved his job. He did nothing all day but tell the other inmates what to do. He could get anything in the facility he wanted, and probably on the outside also. I knew his family on the streets – a couple of his old girlfriends, and some of his hang out locations. It wasn't a problem for him and me to be on opposite teams, because we grew up in the same hood. He never asked me for anything and neither did I ask him for anything. He had occasional run-ins with white officers, wherein matters had to be squashed, or else he would have eventually lost his shopping privileges. I interceded by whispering a word or two in the ear of those officers, and everything was fine.

The thorn in his side that he couldn't shake was Dino. Dino had heard that Stretch had something to do with his people being killed on the outside. Although Dino never confronted Stretch face to face about this, they knew one day that they would be seeing each other. Stretch had a mob of guys behind him, but so did Dino. The funny thing was that Dino was a short, skinny guy when I first became an officer. We used to talk all the time. He started working out like a beast and ate plenty of cakes. I had asked him a while back why he ate so many cakes. He said, "I eat them for the calories." I didn't believe him at first, but what else could cause him to spread out like a tank. You would think that he would try to stop eating so many sweets, because his teeth were deteriorating badly, but I guess he chose muscle over his smile. Anyway, for a couple of nights, I got stuck with doing overtime. I never volunteered to do overtime, because 8 hours was enough in there. Several of us officers had to work the movie detail. We were assigned to the chapel, where we basically stood by the wall. I walked around a little; not too many officers did that, for fear of being struck or grabbed from behind. They seemed frightened or scared to do that. They never seemed to understand the concept of being out-numbered. If you're out-numbered, the inmates could do whatever they wanted to you at any given time. I knew this when I signed up for the job. So, the movie came on and there was a good number of inmates there, but not enough officers. The Muslims were downstairs praying, the inmates upstairs were yelling and my fellow rookie officers were nervous. I thought to myself that if something were to hit the fan, I'd be shit out of luck! The lights were down and all of a sudden I heard, "What, what you gonna do?" I pulled out my flashlight and it was Stretch screaming at Dino! Dino's men stood up and Stretch's guys followed. They were getting closer and closer to each other. Someone pulled the cord on the radio, because I heard, "All officers! Respond to the chapel." The officers came running in with a sergeant who immediately told the officers to cut on the lights and separate the two groups. While Dino's crew was being led out the door, the sergeant turned to me and asked what had happened. I said, "You got me serg."

The next few days were quiet, with the exception of the incident with this guy who thought he was a woman. His fellow inmates kept teasing him. They were chanting, "You're a man, you're a man." He retorted by saying, "No I'm not, I'm a female!" This caused him to rip up the steel plate on his bed and try to castrate himself, so he had to be rushed to the hospital. I didn't care to know the outcome of that ordeal. Anyway, we were all in the gym, which was rather large. There were guys lifting weights in one area and guys running a full court basketball game in another. Everyone was pretty much enjoying their recreational time. Then it happened! An inmate placed two weights in a carry net bag and swung it into another inmate's head. Blood was everywhere! No one seemed to know what happened, with the exception of the guy who was laying on the floor bleeding. The call came once again for the officers to report to the gym, and they came running. This time, they had a medical person with them and he had supplies. The inmate had been knocked unconscious. The medical person was eventually able to bring him back to a conscious state, but he had a gash and a big knot on his head. All I could do was shake my head. It was time to have a meeting, so I sent a kite to Ice. We met and agreed that the two inmates involved in the gym fight needed to get something off their chests, so we set up a fair one. It was set up right before the Thanksgiving holiday; I remember that, because everyone was talking about food. Two officers went to Dino's cell and told him to pack up, because he was being transferred to another prison, and rather quickly. I guess the Warden knew that something huge was about to happen and he wanted to nip it in the bud beforehand. That whole week, guys from Dino's crew were being separated by the transfer. Days later, I saw Stretch and as I approached him he smiled at me. I asked him if he was more at ease since Dino had been transferred. He laughed while saying, "Believe me, he was better off going out that way than the way that I had planned on him leaving!" After Stretch said that, I knew that the Warden had done the right thing by transferring Dino, because if he hadn't, one of them would have wound up dead.

SHORTY NO NECK

Shorty No Neck (Shorty) was like the depiction of his name – he had no neck. He was a fast talker, who mumbled a lot, but I always understood what he was saying. He had a long following, due to his connections in the street, but wasn't a bad guy at all. He always took care of his crew, and would take them shopping during the holiday season. As a result, they always had his back. I remember when Shorty got into an altercation with a guy and one of his people just stiffed the dude. That's loyalty! Shorty and I would converse frequently. He was the kind of guy who you didn't mind being around, especially when you were feeling down and things weren't going too tough. He would always make you laugh by his appearance and the expression on his face. He was like Richard Pryor – you never knew what would come out of his mouth!

One day, while I was doing the headcount, I passed by Shorty's cell and saw him looking at an X-rated magazine. He had the magazine in one hand and his girl's picture in the other. I said, "Shorty, what's good?" He scrambled to put the magazine away, but was still holding the picture. He said, "CO, stop walking up on a mother fucker!" I laughed and said, "What's that in your hand?" He said, "You don't know nothing about this," and gave me the picture to look at. The picture was of a woman lying in bed with her legs up and her insides showing, if you know what I mean. Shorty said, "Yo, this is my heart; she's holding me down. She sends me sh.., makes sure my commissary is on pilot, and takes care of my children. Bet you ain't got nothing like that out there." I said, "Shorty, she sounds like a good woman." Shorty and I always left each other laughing, so I figured that it was my turn to say something crazy. I jokingly said, "The only problem I have is, who took the picture?" Shorty got quite upset and said, "That's some bullshit! I ain't fucking with you CO!" He turned his back to me, walked to his bed and sat there. I knew it was a low blow, but I thought that Shorty would be able to handle anything, being a comedian and all. Apparently not! Weeks went by and every time I saw Shorty in the hall, he would shake his head or throw hand gestures that signified, 'I ain't fucking with you CO.' He was still mad at me, because he wouldn't stop and talk at all. I think I really messed him up!

One afternoon, I opened the gate on the back gallery, just to do my regular security check. I saw several inmates sitting at a picnic table, where they normally play cards and chess. Something was out of the ordinary though, because the gallery was extremely silent. I cautiously approached the inmates to ask what was up. As I did, I saw one inmate with his head turned to a cell. I looked and all I could see was arms and feet, and what appeared to be blood. I rushed to the cell. It was Shorty! He had sliced both of his wrists! I took off my tie while simultaneously pulling the cord on the radio for help. I wrapped my tied around both of Shorty's wrists and applied pressure to the wounds. My hands were bloody, but I wanted to save Shorty's life. The inmates never moved an inch. I guess they thought to themselves that if he wanted to kill himself, let him do it. I wondered to myself if my joking with Shorty about his girlfriend had driven him to this point. Time would definitely tell. My fellow officers finally arrived to put Shorty on a stretcher, and we ran him to the infirmary. Shorty was going to be okay. He was transferred to an outside hospital where he made a full recovery.

Weeks went by and I was assigned to monitor the visiting room. While looking around the room, I noticed Shorty. He was back! A young lady walked up to him and they began hugging each other as if they had just met. They finally sat down and began talking. About 15 minutes passed, and Shorty got out of his seat and came over to me. He said, "There's someone I want you to meet." He walked me over to the young lady and she jumped on me and hugged me saying, "Thank you, thank you, thank you!" I knew what she was talking about then. If it weren't for me, Shorty wouldn't be here. Shorty extended his hand and said, "Thanks CO," and I shook it. I then returned to my post. After a while, it was time for everyone to leave the visiting room, so I made the last announcement. His visitor walked to the left out the door. Shorty walked towards me saying, "You see what I'm saying CO? She's what I'm living for." I nodded my head and said, "My bad Shorty. I didn't realize that my joking would affect you that way." Shorty replied, "It's water under the bridge now CO. We good?" After that, Shorty and I continued to talk often in the Blocks, but I stayed away from any conversation involving his girl, because there was no telling what Shorty would do the next time around.

GATOR

Gator was about 5'9" with broad shoulders. He wore thick glasses and loved to ride his bike. He was a person who tried to make sense of the people in the world. We often tried to figure people out. You see, when you've been in the streets, you come across so many people – some not liking you for the way you smile, some not liking you because of the color of your skin, and some not liking you just because you were born. Those were the kind of conversations that Gator and I used to have when we were in the streets. No matter where I'd be in the boroughs, I would see Gator. I was in a restaurant in Manhattan one day, and guess who I saw passing by the window... Gator! I could have sworn that he was an investigator for the wife or something. LOL. Gator referred to me as L.A. He felt that it was an appropriate name for me, due to the many stories that I had shared with him back in the days. I liked the name, because it gave me a swag.

Some years later, we wound up meeting again at the big house. Gator was a totally different guy then, hanging with these young chain snatchers, although he wasn't that old himself. His crew would steal and rob from the older men and he was their accomplice. I used to hear the old timers yell, "Yeah, they got me, but when I catch them, it's going to be over!" Now I believe that stealing is the worst crime that a man can commit – both inside a prison and outside on the streets. When you're caught stealing, people who hang around you are watching, and although they may not agree with what you're doing, they wind up stealing right along with you. To steal when you're in the streets is one thing, but to do it when you're in prison is just plain wrong, because inmates have minimal supplies in there. Those guys were something else. They were always playing games on the officers. I remember the day when one of them had a problem with a guy on an upper tier. That guy had him jumping the stairs four at a time as he ran for his life. I decided to talk to Gator when I saw him in the gym during recreation. I tried to get him to understand that what he and his guys were doing was wrong. He agreed with me, but not for long, because later on, he and his crew continued to do the same thing.

One morning when I got to work, a member from Gator's crew told me that Gator had went on transit; transit is when you're being transferred to another prison. I asked him where Gator had been transferred to, but he didn't know. Gator's crew had gotten lost; they were all over the place – stealing, getting beaten up and almost murdered. As I was having lunch with my fellow officers later on that afternoon, one of the transit officers came in the Block. He was telling us about an inmate who was transferred to another prison, because he had stolen some goods from some old timers. He had an ID picture of the inmate, so I asked him to let me see it. Sure enough, it was Gator! The card was stamped deceased. All I could say was "Damn! I told him to stop!" I was told that Gator tried to get away with robbing inmates in the prison up north. They referred to up north as across the water. The prisons up there are not like the ones here. The majority of officers up north are white and you are basically alienated. There is no one up there who will have your back, so you're on your own. Those prisons are known for their goon squads and guys go missing in the night. Just ask anybody who has been locked up in the north, and they will tell you that those crackers don't play! I guess Gator found that out the hard way.

It was a day that will ring in prison officials' minds forever. This was the same day that the Correctional Training Academy's teachings would change. On this particular day, officers learned that inmates had a code of their own. As a result, the administration learned to monitor their facilities much closer, officers had to draw the line between friend or foe, and I learned that the power of a man is measured by those who believe in him. You see, fights amongst inmates were considered normal, but an organized fight between an inmate and an officer had never gone down before. This would be the first time in history that this kind of fight would take place.

I have always noticed that when guys are surrounded by other guys, they seem to act different and appear stronger. So, in a correctional environment, you have the inmate who will sometimes taunt the officer or vice-versa. It then becomes a matter of time before one of them gets fed up with the other. He either never wants to see that person again, or he wants that person to stay far away from him. As officers, we were under the impression that we ran the prison, but in all actuality, we were out-numbered. We were in control on the surface, but the truth of the matter is, we were still the minority force, because the ratio of inmate to officer was about 20 to 1. At any given time, we could become a victim, especially in those areas where you are locked in housing units or cubicles, where there are a large number of inmates with only two to three officers. A prime example of this would be the Mess Hall. The Mess Halls in most correctional facilities are huge, holding hundreds of inmates at a time. When fights break out, us officers have been trained to lock the doors and not let anyone out, including your own officers, because you have to isolate the incident. Secondly, officers were to lay on the floor with our hands folded over our heads. That's something that always seemed crazy to me - being trapped in a mess hall with hundreds of inmates who had access to silverware, and I'm lying on the ground! It just didn't seem right!

The dangers of the prison environment didn't actually come from the criminals; at least that's how I felt. Despite the fact that I was amongst murderers, serial killers, rapists and the best of con artists, I never felt like I was in danger. I would sit and talk to the most dangerous of inmates, not caring what they had done. There were prisoners who had killed many and who were involved in massacres, and the more I talked to them, the more I understood, not why they killed, but their mindset at the time of the incidents. Maybe it was my consistency that gave me that edge. I knew that many of those prisoners carried sentences with 100 plus years, and those were the ones that didn't give any problems. The problematic inmates were the ones who committed petty crimes, just so they could get a reputation and make a name for themselves.

There were officers who sometimes came to work with attitudes. They didn't want to be bothered and wod up having a bad day because of that. How could you come to work in a prison environment, with hundreds of inmates, and say you don't want to be bothered? The inmates' main focus is to bother you and get up under your skin. Those officers already knew that, so there was no need for them to complain, because other officers weren't going to feel sorry for them. Some officers complained about their girl and how she was taking their money and hounding them about the long hours being worked. (I can tell you this, I know officers from all walks of life who are never home due to the overtime, and since they weren't spending quality time with their wives, their wives were out there doing their own thing). I believed in fairness. You be fair with me and I'll be fair with you. It wasn't right for an officer to come to work feeling a certain way, because it jeopardized everything we did on that day. I've always felt that the treating of a human being should be fair. I believed that if an inmate was given two cups of fruit, they all should be given an equal amount. If one inmate fought with a shank, then the other should have a shank as well.

So here we go! I was at the door of Sing Sing's Rec Yard and I began the pat and frisk of the officer. I patted him down thoroughly, because I knew very well that we couldn't take a chance with him screwing this up and having it turn into something else. He was anxious and nervous, but ready to squash the beef. He went into the yard alone and I locked him in. When the call for "on the rec" came over the loudspeaker, the inmate who the officer was going to fight came into the Rec

Yard. I frisked and patted him down thoroughly as well. He too was anxious to settle the beef. As I opened the door to let him in, he and the officer began to have words. I said to the both of them, "This is a fair one, a one-on-one; fuck it when you win, or fuck it when you lose; this beef will be over." I quickly locked the door, for fear of someone in the general population hearing the bickering and trying to see what was going on. I glanced through the small 4"X6" window and saw them throwing punches. One was trying to grab the other. I turned from the window to give them time. This is why I believe in the one-on-one; the fair one. Whether it was inmate to inmate, officer to officer, or officer to inmate, it had to go down. (There are only a handful of officers who would be willing to fight alone.) I've observed as some have reacted to different events, while others hesitated until their fellow officers appeared on the scene. Their actions let me know that my back was only protected by a very thin wall, and that wall was referred to as the officer's code. The code was cool until it came down to face-to-face confrontations with prisoners, where only a few would go down swinging. If you were a white officer, my chances were slim to none. If you were a Hispanic officer, I didn't trust that you would back me 100%. If you were black and weren't built for problems, I didn't want you too close to me, because the inmates knew what I was all about; they had an indirect channel to me. They were my eyes, so if something went down and I wasn't around, they would let me know what happened. There were others who were afraid of what the prisoners might do to them if they said a word, but the ones who knew I had their backs kept it 100. Therefore, being asked by one of mine for a one-on-one with a prisoner was not a problem at all, because I knew that he was true to the game.

I also knew that his words were real, so when he asked, I couldn't say no. After all, there were many events that we had participated in during our earlier days, and he never shat on me.

So, back to the fight. I looked into the window again and this time I saw the officer's arm around the inmate's neck. There was blood on the officer's face. The inmate broke out of the chokehold and was trying to pick the officer up to body slam him on the ground. After about 20 minutes, the knock came on the door to the Rec Yard. That knock was from the inmate. When I opened the door, he said, "Thanks; the beef is squashed," and urgently ran off to his cell. I walked into the Rec Yard and looked at the officer. He didn't look good at all! His face had lumps and bruises and blood was everywhere! There was blood on the walls, where it seemed as if the inmate must have rubbed his face against the wall. This was unbelievable to me, because I have seen this officer handle himself in other situations, and in every situation, he had managed to control it. I guess he had met his match this time around. Although the fight lasted for 20 minutes, the officer's face depicted more of an hour! His face looked as if he was in a stick fight and everyone had a stick but him. Unfortunately, the inmate had gotten the best of him. He had really gotten his ass kicked so I had to get him medical attention right away! As we walked out of the Rec Yard down towards the chapel, we saw some officers who asked what had happened. We told them that he had been jumped by an inmate. I escorted him downstairs so that he could clean himself up, while we got our lies together. I said, "You know there's no turning back now; we are in some deep shit. I just need to know how you want to go out." He replied, "I'm good with whatever.

We good?" "Yes," I said, "but I just need to know how you want to go out, because we have to go out together." So, we fabricated a story, a lie, that he got jumped by an inmate in the hallway, and that's what we stuck to. We hadn't weighed the severity of the lie, but either way, we were prepared to go out together, even if it meant doing time. I could tell by the look in his eyes that he was not only hurt physically, but mentally as well. I knew that he was embarrassed too, because he felt like he had let me down. I explained to him that being corrupt comes with its pros and cons. We had adventured together, but now it was over. As the old adage says, "Every dog has his day."

THE PERSUASION
RIKERS ISLAND (THE ISLAND)

At the end of my high school year, I got a job as a counselor at Rikers Island Correctional Institution. This job appeared to be more exciting than any job that I had ever had before. Every day was a new experience. I was fresh out of high school and I got to see criminals locked down for behaviors that I had never seen before. Maybe I shouldn't say that I had never seen before, but it was on a much smaller scale.

I was amazed by the control that the officers had when it came to walking the inmates down the hall. They were paired off in twos, stopping at every corner, every door; this was unbelievable! It wasn't like those shows that you see on television; this was complete control. Every inmate wore the same color jump suit, and there was no talking in the line. It appeared to be the military, until they got back to their cells and holy hell broke loose. There was shouting, dancing, cursing; it was just loud.   I thought to myself, 'Wow, what an environment.' If that didn't prepare you for the real world, what would?

I got along well with the upper brass. It seemed like some of them would come around just to hold conversations with me. We had quite a few laughs together. One of the captains said, "Brister, you're a good man, but if I catch you with one of these women, or hear of you having been with any of them, I will personally lock your ass up!" I replied, "Don't worry, you won't." You see, I was a counselor for the women, so I would be everywhere in the building with them, mainly the gym. They would always come around making passes at me and would try to flirt, but I paid them no mind. A few of them would wear dresses on occasions and they would purposely have their legs open, while playing with the zippers. They did all sorts of freaky things, but it didn't matter, because my mind was straight. I did understand why my captain made that statement though, because the temptation was there. Those were the tolerable aspects of the job, but there was a reverse side that I didn't care for too much. The riots! When riots happened, it would make the hair stand up on the back of your neck. They mostly took place in the recreation yard, where only four or so officers were assigned, amongst an extremely large number of inmates. I remember when a riot broke out one day in the yard and the captain told everyone to lock the gates. The problem was that I and some other officers were on the inside of those locked gates. All you could see were fists flying and we had to remain backed against the gate for a while. The situation was soon resolved and inmates were cuffed and taken away, but what a hell of an experience for someone coming out of high school. I guess this is what led me to work in that type of environment.

OFFICER DOWN (CODE BLUE)

There's nothing worse than being locked in a facility and not being able to go home! It was first said by Dorothy, in the "Wizard of Oz", that "There's no place like home." Oh wow! How I wish I'd never left home that day! There's a terrible feeling that comes over you when you know that you caused something to happen and that you're now responsible for it. You see, all of us officers carried walkie-talkies and connected to the walkie-talkie was a response cord. If that cord is pulled, officers will respond in numbers. On this particular day, they weren't coming due to an inmate having a problem; they were coming because an officer had started a problem. Yeah, I knew that I was in deep shit and that I would probably lose my job and be arrested, but in any event, I was going to walk out of that facility with my head held high. I had always been taught that as a man, you are responsible for your actions, so I was prepared to roll with the punches and face the consequences. After all, this was prison, the big times. I thought about the prison prostitution ring that had been shut down years earlier. The female officers who were involved in that operation were led out of the prison one by one in handcuffs, and not one of them had their head held down. They took responsibility for what they had done, so I couldn't let them show me up by not doing the same. If I ever had a guardian angel, I needed that angel now!

I've heard people say over the years that if they were in any given situation, they would do this or they would do that, but the truth of the matter is, you really don't know what you'd do until you are actually faced with that situation. What you do is who you are, so when these particular situations arise, you will find strength that you never knew you had. I have seen men shooting and trying to kill other men, and when they were brought in front of the system, they broke down and cried. If they had listened to their hearts, which never lies, instead of their heads, they would have never committed the crime. I do understand that in every man there's something within that cries out for them to 'be bad, go ahead and do it, don't worry about anything, take the consequences as they come,' but they have to realize that in prison, it's either going to be a good time or a bad time. A good time would mean that, according to who they knew, their sentence would be a piece of cake, but a bad time would mean that that they'd have to do hard time, according to who they had screwed in the streets. They would also have to be constantly looking over their shoulders. So, think before you act, because this is not the path that you want to take. Impulsive thinking is how criminals are made and how people are killed. You would then be faced with a life sentence as you sit back, like those notorious ones before you, and say to yourself, 'If I could do it all over again, I would do things differently, but now it's too late.'

THE OUTSIDE HOSPITAL RUN

We had made this trip many times before, but this time it was different. The outside hospital run was designed so that the officers could transport inmates on medical runs. We would take them to the hospital and would have to sit there with them. You rarely ran into a situation where an inmate tried to escape, but if he did, we were equipped to take care of him. While at the hospital, there were times when family members tried to intervene in our correctional work or procedures, but we let them know that we had direct orders from the facility, so they would have to take their concerns up within the prison, not us. In some instances, the inmate died at the hospital, and it became a very sensitive situation, because his family wanted to exert their anger somewhere, so why not on an officer. I had been to the hospital for many different cases, but this particular case was brought on by me. The sergeant that drove us to the hospital received a call from the Warden that a certain officer was missing. It was said that this particular officer had escaped the facility. The sergeant asked for the name of the missing officer, and the Warden gave him my name! The Warden told the sergeant that he wanted this officer (me) back in the facility ASAP! The sergeant was a friend of mine and he said, "Listen, I need to know what happened so that I can protect you." I said, "Serg, there's nothing you can do. I have to go out like this." He replied, "I can fix this." I told him that I knew we had done a lot together and that I could always count on him to help me, even it meant him taking the fall, but this fall was mine to deal with. We shook hands and he ordered the other officer, who was in the car with us, to drive me back to the facility.

Upon my return to the prison, a great lockdown was in progress! I had seen lockdowns before, but never of this magnitude; it was crazy! As I looked up, I saw the Warden standing there, looking like a giant, with his chest puffed out. He was 6'5" tall, but on this day, he seemed to stand about 7' or better. He was looking at me as if to say, 'You're going down. I'm going to make an example of you.' (The thing with me is this, I get fed up once I've reached a certain point, and then I come to a place of no return. Once I come to that place of no return, there is nothing that can be done to me, and everything that I expect to happen, probably will happen.) Some people may want to see you cave in and cry or die, but I'm not that guy. In the end, when the punches are thrown, I want them to know that I'll throw back! I am a soldier who would rather die on his feet than on his knees. I said all of that to say that although the Warden had me in the right, and I didn't have a leg to stand on, I was going to keep my chin up. I had already felt the prejudices that the prison held against people of a different persuasion, so I knew that the worst was yet to come. I was accompanied by two other officers as we marched straight to the Warden's office. I guess they came along to ensure that I didn't beat the Warden down or try to run. Running was the furthest thing from my mind. Besides that, the Warden was the one with the key. I knew what I had done and I was willing to face the consequences.

- CHAPTER 8 -

THE INTERROGATIONS

It had been a long day and now it was dark. My shift was over and going home was not in the plan, because the facility had plans for me of their own. The plan was to make sure that I left the prison in handcuffs, so calls were made and other agencies got involved. One in particular was the New York State Police, who had to investigate the event. The officers from that agency came in one by one, as I sat in the Warden's office in a chair next to his desk. The Warden left and gave them the room. I looked at both of the officers and said to myself, 'Stay in the zone. Remember, they are officers and they'll probably be the only ones to help me out of this mess.' As the first officer began to ask questions, I recounted the lie that we had made up in the basement of the chapel, that an inmate had jumped my partner in the hallway. We went through numerous questions – what happened, being the first. The story was perfect, although I knew that the job was to find the truth. I knew that they would investigate the Rec Yard, the hallway, the inmates, and the officer involved in the fight. I knew that they were going to try to turn me against him and him against me. The truth of the matter is, all those officers were concerned about was their jobs. We were interrogated for hours, from one officer to the other, but my partner and I stood firm in our story and didn't allow them to intimidate us. Our story was solid, and they had to prove that we were lying.

The State Attorney General then walked into the room! This was huge, because in order for the State Attorney General to come all the way from Albany, it had to be something very serious! It didn't mean much to my partner and me though, because we were sticking to our story. The Attorney General was a female. I was sort of wishing that she would've been a male instead of a female, because men normally look at each other to decipher whether the person is telling the truth, but women automatically sense if you're guilty, no matter what you say or do. At least that's what I believe. Anyway, she began asking me questions. She asked me for my nightstick. "What does my nightstick have to do with this?" She replied," I was told that it was you who beat the officer down." "Wow!" I said, as I gave it to her. I had rubber bands wrapped around the stick for a better grip. She said that they were wrapped around so thick until they wouldn't leave a mark. Ain't this some shit! I knew she was serious now, so I had to up my game. She began drawing up papers, so in the interim, I asked her if I could go to the men's room. She obliged me. I ran down to the officer's locker room and who did I see but Stone, my co-defendant. I explained to him that we were going to take a fall and I asked him how he wanted to go out. Now, Stone knew how powerful I was, so he had no choice but to say that he was with me and whatever happens, happens. It was going to be the officer's code to the end. The officer's code was to stick together, no matter what. So, we devised a plan to signal a tap or whatever we could do to keep the story going.

I returned to the uncomfortable wooden chair in front of the Attorney General. She smiled, although there had been no joke, so I knew that she had something on me. (Unbeknownst to me, while I was being interrogated by the State Attorney, the State Police were examining the areas in which the fight had occurred). She said, "Tell me what happened today, from the time you woke up this morning until now." I broke it down to her - from breakfast to the incident, with a curve, of course. She said, "Are you sure that that's how it went?" I replied, "Yes". She also threatened me with 15 years of State time. I said, "Unless you can find proof of me beating an officer down, or even throwing a punch, then you have nothing!" She then pulled out a federal document and told me to read and sign it. The paper had my exact words on it, but I refused to sign them.

In the meantime, Officer Stone was now being interviewed in the other room. As the door opened and he walked through, we tapped each other to signify that the code was still good. So now it was time for me to go through the door and speak to the State Police again, but wait a minute, I didn't get a tap from Stone! 'Wow!' I thought to myself. 'Maybe he forgot! Damn! I wonder if this nigga gave us up.' I was sitting in the chair, trying to look through a closed door to see his expression, a sign or something, but there was no way for me to see through that door. "So", said the State Police officer, "We know what happened." Now it came to the good cop, bad cop routine. One officer was polite and said, "If I were in this type of mess, I would want you to back me up. The other officer said, "Let's wrap this up; we have what we need." I could only figure that something must have been found, something that proved to them where the fight had actually taken place. "Look, we know what happened to your partner; he told us everything. If you don't believe me, look in the next room at your partner's face. That should prove to you that we know." I stood firm as I looked at my partner's face. He held his battered face down as if to say that he had to tell the truth. The officers told me a whole lot, but I still wasn't willing to snitch on my partner. "I'm going to name an item," said the officer, and that item will tell you that we know what happened and where it happened." I said, "Okay, let me hear what you know." He said, "The same watch that you were wearing was found in the Keep Lock Recreational Yard, along with blood scrapes on the walls." When he said watch, I felt my ass shrink up like a raisin! Damn, he gave us up! At this point, I knew that they had me! Stone had obviously told them where the fight was. I sat down and listened to the rest.

The documents soon surfaced again. I refused to sign anything, but decided to give my own statement. Apparently, there must have been a whole lot of inmates who saw what happened and they were all too eager to tell the State Police what had happened. They had all of the information now – who did it, the participants and the controller. The other officer told me to stand up with my hands behind my back. He grabbed my left hand as his partner walked to the door. When he opened the door, I saw Stone and he didn't look like a guy who was staying true to the code, but I still gave him the benefit of the doubt. The officer said, "Look at your partner. We promised him 15 years and he rolled." We will promise you the same. I told him to put the other cuff on. When they hit Stone with those 15 years, he had to fold. He had held it down for as long as he could, but facing 15 years for some Bull Shit, I guess he said, 'Hell no!'

The state police officer told me that he didn't want to shame me by having me walk through the halls in handcuffs, with my peers looking on, so he allowed me to walk in front of him. He was a good dude. I arrived at the State Police Headquarters and they began the fingerprinting process. I was questioned once again, and this time I had to tell the truth. I really didn't want to tell the truth, because it meant revisiting the act once again.

CONFISCATION OF WEAPONS

I was released to go home, with a pending trial, under the supervision of my lawyer. A couple of days had passed by and I hadn't seen or heard from anyone. I stayed to myself and tried to collect my thoughts. One afternoon, as I was going down into the basement where my brother lived, the phone rang. I picked it up and it was the Attorney General's office. What could they want now? They already have my ass in the palm of their hand! The voice on the other end said, "Pursuant to directive number 2020 off duty firearms regulations, you are hereby warned that effective immediately, you may not carry a firearm by virtue of your peace officer standards, while off-duty, until further notice." I knew then that my guns had to be turned into the arsenal, all except for two, (which my close friend was going to take) by Tuesday morning, or a warrant would be issued for my arrest, so I agreed to turn them in. At this point, I trusted no one, but I called up my close comrade and said, "I need you to do something for me. It's very important; a matter of life and prison time." He said, "OK. Whatever you need." I replied, "Monday morning, before you go to work, stop by here. I need you to check my weapons into the arsenal." "You got it," he said. When Monday morning came, he pulled up with a duffel bag. We placed the weapons in the bag and I told him to make sure that he got a receipt when he turned the weapons in. I asked him to bring the receipt to me on his way home and stressed to him how important this was. Later on that day he dropped the receipt off to me. I was good now!

On Tuesday morning I got up and went for a jog. I had been pretty tense, so I figured that I'd try to start relaxing a bit. When I came back from jogging, I got a little breakfast going and then washed my car. I was chilling, but I still had this incident hovering over my head. The day went by quickly and around 6:00 p.m., the phone rang. I answered it and the voice said, "Is this Mr. Brister?" I said, "Yes." He said, "This is the office of the Attorney General. A warrant has been issued for your arrest." I said very excitedly, "What for? You people told me to check my weapons into the arsenal and I did!" I gave him the day and time of the check-in. "Ya'll need to find someone else to harass, because I'm not putting up with this Bull Shit!" I abruptly hung up the phone! As it turned out, they had apparently made a mistake, because they had never checked the arsenal. I found this out later on when I put in a speed dial call to my attorney.

ARBITRATION

On the day of arbitration, there was only one thing to do –

walk into the room with my head up, chest out, look them straight in the eyes, and take the punches. After all, what else could they do to me? Besides, I already knew that arbitration was nothing more than a face-to-face meeting with your boss, so that he could mumble obscenities under his breath, and look into the face of the person who tried to destroy his program. I was a firm believer that every dog has his day and this one was mine. So, they began asking questions about what I had done. They already knew the answers, but they just wanted to see if they could broaden my notice of discipline, you know, add on more misconduct to the charges. They knew that I was no dummy, because I had done this for years, undetected, so what did that make them? I listened to the disciplinary charges, and boy were there many. They had misconduct in sections that I had never seen before. It seemed as if they had put subtitles on top of subtitles. If you could have read my reasons for discipline, you would have said, "Damn!"

Then came the conduct and activities of the employee. There were more charges added under those charges. So now comes my statement, you know, the lie. The problem with the statement was that I didn't write like that; it wasn't my wording. Okay. I saw what this was; it was hang a nigga day! I said to them, "If you have all of this, then you know my direction, so what am I doing here?" They stopped for a minute and looked at each other, knowing that I was right. I stood up, turned my back on them and walked out. I wasn't taking anymore directives, memos, or meetings. This was it for me. If they wanted to roast a nigga, I wasn't going to hang around to help them start the fire. Everything was pending upon the outcome of the court case, and I already knew what the outcome was going to be.

As a side bar, when I walked into the arbitration room, I expected to be treated a certain way, although I didn't have any representation present. I did have a union rep who said that he was going to fight for me by finding grounds to stand on and eliminate all doubts. Well, as time progressed, he became ill. At one point, when I met with him, I was afraid to shake his hand. I don't know what disease he was carrying, but he had visible sores on his face and hands, and I wasn't about to shake his hand. I believe he said to me that he was dying. Back then, when a person was ill with those symptoms, people thought one thing. He had the monster. Now you know why he wasn't with me when I walked into the arbitration room.

- CHAPTER 9 -

ADMINISTRATION ATTACKS

The prison officials wanted me to be arrested so bad until they didn't care how it took place, so they were conjuring up all kinds of attempts to get me in that 4X4 cell. They wanted me to hurt just as much as I had made others hurt.

It had been a rough week, so I had planned the night before to get up early and go for a run. It was a beautiful day that next morning and I couldn't wait to hit the park. I worked out as I usually did and it was great. With the incident pending in my mind, I needed stress relievers, so working out was the best thing for me, since I didn't drink or smoke. I tried to let most things roll off my back, without thinking about what had transpired. I needed to carry myself forward by seeking other means of employment right away. I was glad when Chase Manhattan Bank called for me to be a debt collector! Things were going well with Chase Manhattan Bank. I was meeting new people while learning a new trade and I was able to place the past in the back of my mind. But then it happened again! I got a call from my brother, who was a New York State police officer. He told me that the two guns that I had signed over to him had to be melted down and that the facility had no record of them ever being turned in. He also told me that he was being suspended from work for two weeks for possessing an illegal handgun. I would in no way put his family in harm's way, so this was just another attempt by the system to try to railroad me. I believe that my friend knew what was going on, but he didn't want to go into it, due to our tight relationship. I knew that another attack was soon to follow, because I was called into the office by the bank manager and was questioned about my employment with Sing Sing Correctional Facility. I told him that everything he needed to know was on my application. He told me that if I didn't explain to him right then and there what had happened with my last employer, I would have to leave, so I got up and walked out! I knew what this was all about! A few days later, I was at a friend's funeral and was confronted by a former co-worker from Chase Manhattan Bank. She asked me why I had left. I told her that some of my past history had caught up with me. She said, "I don't know if you know this or not, but after you left the bank, it was robbed, and guess whose picture was being shown around. I looked at her, smiled and told her that this was just another case of my past trying to overwhelm my future.

The attack came once again when I was hired by the United States Department of Immigration and Naturalization Service. This job was to detain illegal immigrants in a prison setting. Things were going well once again, as I was meeting more new people and enjoying the power of the badge. We frequently transported detainees to numerous countries. I became favorable with my superiors, because of my build and the way I spoke. When an outside detail came up, the chief of operations, as well as the officers, wanted me with them. A new family had evolved for me, but instead of wearing blue, we wore green, which represented a different code. The detainees wore yellow. The detainees were also of a criminal nature, waiting to be deported to another country. Some of the problems that we encountered were with countries who either wouldn't accept them, or countries who felt that they disgraced them and wanted to execute them, so we had to find a country that would accept them. Most of the time, they stayed in the holding area for months. This was the same environment as that of a prison. We carried guns and watched over them just as I had done with the criminals in prison.

One day, after two years of service, I was about to be sent to Langley, but I was summoned to the office. It was evident to me that my reputation was flawless, and I had received numerous awards for my service, so I didn't know why I was being called upon. When I was asked to have a seat, it was something that I knew all too well. Then the questions began. "Tell me about your employment at Sing Sing Correctional Facility." (Now mind you, I'm a person who will sit back and collect my attitude and personality before I answer you). The person who was doing the questioning was an old dried up Uncle Tom, who just needed something to do to keep him going. His name was Leroy, a debilitated ass nigga, who always sat behind a desk. He kept his distance from us officers, because he was afraid that one of us might one day tare the lining out of his ass! When this house nigga got wind that something was wrong in my file, he wanted me out, so the questions came in all forms and fashion. I was asked about my actions in Sing Sing and why the administration was never informed. Bear in mind, this was the federal government, and I had worked there for over two years without being questioned. The federal government's application at that particular time was over ten pages long, and the investigations were thorough, so there was no way that they could have overlooked my answers to all of their questions I knew what was going down, but I wasn't about to give them the satisfaction of the doubt.

That night, as I returned home, I decided that if this was going to be another attack, which it was, I would make the first move. I decided to devise a plan to resign, so I typed up my resignation letter in duplicate and sent one via overnight mail to the chief. I knew what might have been lurking in the air, because that Leroy character didn't like me one bit after my visitation with him the other day, so I knew that he was going to ask the Department of Justice to downgrade me. That feeling of not being in the dark about anything was always a good one. I was going to be prepared this time around. I was tired of the uneasiness I had been feeling, the butterflies in my stomach, the headaches and the droopy eyes.

The next day was a normal, but very long workday. Like every day before, immigration officers stood around talking to inmates and to each other. Some snuck in a game of chess, checkers or got a piece of ass in the visiting room. Others stood along the walls, just waiting for their day to end. A few of the officers really didn't want to go home, because this was their excitement.

As evening approached, I was working a special unit and in this unit that housed approximately seven detainees, I heard over the intercom, "Will the officer on Post 7 report to the chief?" This was it! No longer would I be set up! This time around, I was going to set myself up! As I approached the chief, who believed in me and always wanted me around, he handed me an overnight mail package. I said, "Chief, it's not for me; it's for you." You see, I addressed it to myself, knowing that you would call me into our office." He asked, "What is this about?" I replied, "Chief, it's a long story. It's been wonderful, and this is the end of the road for me. Today is my last day." You should have seen the look on his face! I knew a resignation had never been orchestrated toward him like this before. I explained to him that I had been blackballed and attacked for the past couple of years, but this time around, I wasn't going to give anybody the benefit of the doubt. He seemed to understand as we shook hands. I then slid into the darkness, saying to myself that this was the right way to do it.

THE ATTORNEY FIGHTS FOR MY FREEDOM
COURT PROCEEDINGS

Like any good criminal, you need a good attorney. Stephen James was that for me. He was a one in a million kind of attorney. He seemed to be more interested in me as a person than he was in the money or what I had done. If you've ever dealt with an attorney, you know that in order to become a great attorney, you have to have a wonderful life. Your morals, values, and everything along that nature, has to be kept in perspective. Those characteristics help to make attorneys great. Mr. James seemed to want what I had, but I wasn't exactly sure what it was that he wanted. I wondered what it was that was causing him to draw close to me. Did he have a desire within to be a criminal, or was he looking for someone to teach him the streets? Well, only time would tell.

My case started off as a court proceeding. I would first meet the judge and the judge would determine if I would have to do time for what I had done. The court was in the town of Ossining, NY. Those towns were not like the one I lived in; they were suburban and of the Caucasian persuasion, so the strikes were already against me. The ride to court that day was as usual, mainly because it was like my ride to work every morning. The only difference was that it was a little further down the road. I parked my car in an area for parking all day, because I didn't know if I was going to be released, or if I would have to do time. If I had to do time, I would have family come and pick my car up. The courthouse was your typical everyday court environment: lawyers with expensive suits were walking the halls, jurors who had been called for jury duty were waiting for their names to be called, police were coming in and out, and criminals were trying to get off or awaiting their sentencing. I knew which stance I had to take. It's a very uncomfortable feeling when you're all alone and don't know if you're going to be incarcerated the next minute. It feels like your body is going to go numb to everything around you.

At long last, my name was called by the judge. I approached the bench and the judge asked me if I could afford an attorney. I guess the charges were so severe that without an attorney, the judge felt like I wouldn't have a chance. I told the judge that I wasn't in a position to afford an attorney, and asked if I'd be able to request a court appointed attorney. The judge handed me a form and told me to fill it out. I walked into the hallway to complete it.   It asked for all of my financial information, which I just happened to have on me. 'Yeah right,' I said to myself. I was smart enough to know that if I provided all of my financial information that I wouldn't be eligible for a court appointed attorney, but I filled out the paperwork just the same and submitted it. Just as I figured, I was told that I wasn't eligible for a court appointed attorney. I was also told that my case had been postponed for a later date. This was good, because I would now have time to acquire an attorney. I contacted Attorney Stephen James, who agreed to take my case for a minimum amount of money. He believed that the case wasn't as bad as they said it was. He knew the law and the court system, so I entrusted him with my case by telling him the truth – that I did it all.

You would expect that an attorney, who grew up in a different environment than yourself, would be one to look down at you, or frown upon what you had done. That wasn't the case with Attorney James though. He was different. He seemed more down to earth; he was more like me. So, on the day of the hearing, he defended me as if I was his brother. He was the absolute truth. At one point, the judge asked me a question, which I couldn't answer, but Attorney James took it from there and hit him with a hard response. Attorney James responded to the point where the judge couldn't even give a reasonable reply. I stood there and said to myself, 'This man knows his stuff.' The judge was so embarrassed and had no other choice but to drop the charge and reduce it to a misdemeanor, which was nothing. I paid the fine and walked away a free man!

I needed to know just who Attorney James really was, and I guess he needed to know who this guy was who he had just defended and who got off. It seemed that we both admired what the other had. I admired him for being a young attorney and he admired my ability to maneuver people's thoughts in given situations. So, this meant that it was time for us to become boys. We started hanging out together on my turf. I introduced him to my team and my hangout spots, and he in turn introduced me to a high caliber of people. The *Al Sharptons*, the radio personalities, up and coming artists, etc. He brought out a side of me that I never knew existed. I guess that we both had a yearning for the other one's life. He knew of my power in the prisons, and I knew of his power in the court system, so we became a great team!

When I was at the Downstate Correctional Facility, a kite came to me from the streets saying that there was an inmate there who was using Attorney James' name for scam purposes. I told Attorney James about it and he said that we needed to take care of it immediately. He and I drove two hours to the Fishkill Correctional Facility. We parked in front of the building and he ran in to see the inmate who was fraudulently using his name. I guess he must have hit him with some real bad shit, because he no longer had to worry about this inmate. He thanked me for informing him and told me that whatever is his is mine. He appreciated the way I always looked out for him and he reciprocated by doing the same for me. This brought about a true friendship – the kind of friendship where you could leave this guy with your girl and not have to worry about him making any moves. It was the kind of friendship where we were always there for each other, no matter what, because we were boys!

It was strange to have a guy fight to keep you out of prison, and then become your closest friend. I was glad to have that relationship with Attorney James though. We had similar street preferences – he liked crime, because he got paid for the cases; I liked crime, because basically, I was a criminal. He also liked nice cars and so did I. I would hit him up quite often to use his car. Attorney James was a ladies man and was referred to as Johnny. He swore that he was handsome and, well, you can figure out the rest. He was a rather clever guy in the streets and a beast in the courtroom! Once again when I had accompanied him to court, the judge asked him a question, and his response caused the judge to have to look it up in a book! "Damn," I said to myself. I guess it's cool to know your stuff. Johnny gravitated towards me due to my people skills. I have always had a special skill to converse with anyone, anyplace and anywhere. I basically read people's body language – the movement of their arms, head and I can surmise their stress levels by doing so. This has been my training throughout life. What Johnny didn't know was that I had been trained by the streets. I grew up with guys who had spent numerous years in prison. For example, Mike went to prison for 13 years for robbing an armored car in the 80's. Tee had done 15 years for robbery. So many guys who I had walked with, talked with, ate with and drank with on a daily basis were criminals. Most of them had moved out of New York after committing a serious crime. Toni was one guy who had committed so many murders. He left New York, but then returned years later. I happened to run into him one day on Jamaica Avenue. I asked him what he was doing here. He said that he loves New York and had to come back every once in a while to visit. We shook hands and I walked away. I have learned not to be anywhere around those guys, because there was always someone lurking around to take them out. Also, there were guys who I knew that used to hustle. I respected them and they respected me. I would talk to them for a little while, but I had to get up out of there when unfamiliar faces approached them.

Let me tell you about the time when I used to hang out in the clubs. On this particular day, Johnny wasn't available to come with me, so I took another partner of mine named Rob. Rob had just gotten out of a little 2 to 3-skid bid, and he needed some money, so I hired him to work with me. When evening came, we decided to go to a club named Wedge in the Bronx. This wasn't an ordinary club. We were shooting pool in this club, and there were many ladies there, who were getting their drinks. Rob asked me to hold his drink for him while he went to the men's room, so I did. If you've ever been in the Wedge, you know that there is only one way in and one way out – through the front door. After a while, the front door opened and a mob of guys came walking through. In front of them was a Spanish guy, who seemed to be the one in charge. This guy, who I had never seen before, walked straight up to me with his entourage and they basically surrounded me. He put his left hand around my shoulder and said, 'I appreciate that shit you did last night." I looked at him and smiled, not knowing what the hell he was talking about. He said, I'm going to buy you a drink. What you drinking?" "Hennessey," I said. He said, "Cool," and walked to the bar as his entourage followed. Rob had seen the guys surrounding me when he came out of the bathroom and asked me what that was all about. I said, "I don't know, but when I hit the door, if you're not right behind me, I'm leaving you in here." We both dashed to the door so fast until we might have torn it down! We got to the car, jumped in and raced back to Queens. I never did find out what that guy was talking about, but I can bet you one thing, the way the hair was standing up on the back of my neck, I knew that they were planning to do me in that night! You see, you don't have to know a whole lot about the environment that you live in, but what you need to know is when to get the hell up out of there. This might be one of the things that Johnny knew about me. Soon after that incident, Johnny and I fell distant. Tragedy struck his home and we fell off, but I still have much love for that dude.

We live in a world where it's to your benefit to know for sure if your brother is really your brother's keeper, and if he has got your back. Most people can say that I've never done them wrong and that I've always had their back, but unfortunately, I can't say the same.

- CHAPTER 10 -

STREETS TALK
FOOD FOR THOUGHT

I have never said that I was at all innocent. How could I be innocent if I knew what was going down? Some look at the world and say to themselves, 'What is the problem with others?' There are others who look at the world and say to themselves, 'What is the problem with me?' I really don't think I have a problem. I just think that the same environment that I grew up in became a part of me. I love all that I have written. I have expressed parts of my life and events, which have made me the man I am today. I have expressed the hurts, the pains and some of the people who were the most impressionable to me. I have learned that you don't ever really know people, for the simple fact that at any given situation, people may change. I can go back to as far as having my first bike stolen. I knew that the chances of it being stolen was a great possibility, since I had left it parked outside of a store, but I left it out there anyway. I also knew that growing up with people who were not in my best interest would either tarnish my life or make me stronger. Life's events will mold you into who you are. If you've never experienced love, you won't know what hate is. You need to experiment for yourself to see what suits you.

I knew that my hanging out in the wee hours of the morning, having to climb into a window to get into the house was wrong. I knew that waving guns at people and making people submit was wrong. I knew that racing my car down a one-way street over 90 mph was wrong. I knew that stealing cars for joy rides was wrong. I knew that being a part of a gang and treating people a certain way was wrong. The only reason that I know all of this now is because I'm older. In the past, I had never stopped to consider the feelings of others, because I just didn't care. I can now look back over my life and tell my kids stories, hoping that they will care for others more than I did.

You also need to understand that on average, most people aren't trying to hurt you, they just want to be connected to you. They're looking for a smile, for someone to open the door for them, for someone to show a little love. It's like going into the job market. The jobs that last the longest are the ones that you have prepared yourself for. If you're interested in helping people, you might seek a job in the healthcare department. If you're interested in protecting people, you may get a job in the field of law enforcement. What if you don't like working for people, but you like working around people? Perhaps you will start your own business venture, wherein you will have the control of seeing people at your own discretion.

There's a whole lot to learn in these streets. There are people who will love you for who you are, or just because of the way you walk. On the other hand, there are people who will hate you just because you look the way you do. It's not easy in the world out there, especially for men. Most men feel that as soon as they walk out the door, they have to put on this Mr. Macho image – something that can be taken away with a simple slap in the face. There are other men who will take your life just because they don't want to see you anymore. Then you have the ones who believe that they own the streets – everything that moves and every person that talks. The only thing that I can say to that is, as sure as you and I bleed, they will too. You hear many things on the streets, but only if you listen carefully. There are those who walk the streets as zombies, never seeing what's on the side of them, and never seeing 6 feet in front or to the rear of them. There are also other human beings who want no contact with other humans. Can you believe that? Anyway, the fact of the matter is that if you or your parents were raised in an environment which exerted a certain kind of energy, then nine out of ten times, someone in your family will have that energy. I wouldn't say that their metabolism was fast, or that they were necessarily a screw up, but they would probably be more of a risk-taker and would utilize that energy for adventure or excitement. Also, know that if that energy isn't harnessed properly, it could create problems in your future.

- CHAPTER 11 -

DREAMS

There were many nights when I would awaken in a cold sweat, thinking of what had happened and the future that was to come. The thing about the dreams was that they always started in this one place and ended in the same place, give or take a scene or two. But like anything you practice, whether you're a teacher, preacher, play sports, or an intense fan on the sidelines, you will dream of that particular thing that you put so much energy into. The job became a high-energy job for me. My energy level at one time was to the point where I wanted things to happen, so that we could respond or react to a situation, somewhat like the new jacks who graduated from the Police Academy. Those new jacks were fresh out of the academy with on-the-job training and wanted to do something. They wanted something that would give them an edge for a promotion, so that their fellow officers would look up to them. They too cared to dream, but they dreamed of power, of carrying a gun, of wearing a uniform, and of gaining respect. It's like I previously said, when you become a member of the team, you gain power. You lose on that idea of being a host to God and become a hostage to your own ego.

That power becomes addictive and with that addiction comes the thirst. At one point or another, you must quench that thirst. The over-addicted ones are always the ones to fall first.

Note to self:

Michael De Montaigne once said, "Dreams are the true interpretations of our inclinations, but Art is required to sort and understand them."

- CHAPTER 12 -

SPIRITS, GHOSTS, STRANGE EVENTS

Most people will say that they don't believe in spirits or ghosts, and that's cool. I was one of those people, until I experienced it myself. In 1986, my family and I relocated to Poughkeepsie, NY where the houses were probably over 100 years old. Now, I know that things could happen even if the house was only 10 years old, but 100 years is a long time, so there's no telling what kinds of events transpired in that timeframe.

One night, my mind wouldn't let me sleep, so I got out of the bed, so as not to disturb my wife. I was anxious, leery, and felt as if something was about to happen. Old folks would generally say that your restlessness was probably due to something that you ate, something that you had on your mind, or that you were in some type of trouble. It wasn't any of those things for me, but I just couldn't figure out why I was feeling that way. I went to lay back down in the bed with my wife, who slept near the wall with the window at her feet. I always slept facing the door, because this was a means of security for her, and it made me feel like I was protecting my family. I soon fell asleep, and only got up once for a bathroom run and to look out the front window. I still had a gut feeling that something wasn't right though. On the way back from the front window, I checked all three bedrooms. (We had gotten this three-bedroom apartment for a bargain at $300 a month, something that was unheard of, so we snatched it up real quick).

Since I was still feeling anxious, I locked my bedroom door, because in the instance that something were to happen, I would at least have time to get to my weapons. After a while, I fell asleep again, but not without a lot of tossing and turning; I eventually ended up on my back. I didn't sleep long, because I was awakened by a figure in a white dress, who I knew couldn't have opened my bedroom door, because I had locked it. As the figure got closer and closer, I could see that it was a white lady with gold looking hair. I could not move! I was paralyzed! She wasn't going away; she wanted to see me up close! Her face came closer and closer to mine, as I tried reaching for my wife, but then she disappeared into thin air! It was as if she was never there! I got up, unlocked my bedroom door and checked the front and back doors. I then checked every room in the apartment, looking for what I had seen. That was incredible! The problem was, would I tell anyone or keep it to myself? I decided to keep it to myself!

There was another time when I ran into something that wasn't supposed to be there. It happened when I was younger and we were living in a large house, which sat in the center of the block. The house was popular, because when it rained, a giant pool of water formed in front of the house like a swimming pool. We knew all of the neighbors, because when they passed by our house, they had to hold onto the gate to keep from falling into the large body of water. We enjoyed telling the neighbors to hold on, while watching their faces light up with smiles. It was a particularly cold night, and my brothers and I had been out playing for hours until we were exhausted. It was now time to go to sleep. Mom called up to the third level, the attic, and said, "Boys, it's time for bed." Mom didn't play, so when she said it was time for bed, it was time for bed! There were two beds in our room. The one on the left side belonged to my two younger brothers and the one on the right belonged to me. The moonlight shined through a single window at the head of the beds. At the foot of the beds was a chimney that sat in the middle of the floor. The only way out of the room was to go around the chimney on either side. I had never had a problem with sleeping, but for some reason, on this night, it wasn't easy. I eventually drifted off to sleep though. From a young age, I had tried to teach myself to wake up when I was in certain situations, like falling off of something, being chased, or when you know you're about to be killed. It was training for me and I became good at it. This uneasy feeling made me open my eyes, and when I did, it seemed as if I saw something moving on the other side of the chimney. I stayed still and acted as if my eyes were closed. I saw this little man on one side of the chimney with a green hat glancing at me and then at my brothers. I told myself that as soon as he turns again, I would make a run for it, right around the opposite side of the chimney. He'd have to snatch me to catch me. As soon as he turned again, I went flying pass the chimney, taking the stairs four or five at a time. Your parents' room is probably the safest place to run to when your world has been turned upside down, so there I went, and sat at the bottom of their bed. In a few moments, mom called my name. She said that she had called me several times, but I only heard her once. Pop woke up and looked at me in a certain way as if to say, 'My son must have seen something.' They told me that I must have been dreaming, so go back to sleep, and I did.

Years later, I heard my mom telling a story of what had happened to her. She said that she was in the kitchen and pop was in the bedroom sleeping. She said she saw a little man with a hat on, dangling a knife over my pops' stomach, and as she screamed, he disappeared. The entities were similar, so was it something that was after my father, but had now decided to go after me? Well, all I know is that if something is out there, Pop is no longer with us, so the buck stops with me!

LEAVE MY SON ALONE!!!

A MESSAGE FROM THE AUTHOR

This South Queens prison story is true. The names of the individuals involved were protected, due to ongoing beefs, as well as administrative attacks. I should know!

Note to self:

A famous political figure once said that we on this side are praying to him to give us victory, cause we believe we are right; those on the other side prayed to him too, for victory, believing that they are right. So, what must he think of us?

Famous quotes that are now the essence of my being...

One friend in a lifetime is much; two are many; three are hardly possible. Friendship needs a certain parallelism of life, a community of thoughts, a rivalry of aim.
– **Henry Adams**

People hate those who make them feel their own inferiority.
– **Lord Chesterfield**

Whom men fear, they hate, and whom they hate, they wished dead. – **Quintus Ennius**

Better a thousand times to die with glory than live without honor. – **Louis VI of France**

Mine honor is my life, but grows in one; Take honor from me and my life is done. – **Shakespeare**

Wise men learn much from their enemies.
– **Aristophanes**

He makes no friend who never made a foe. – **Tennyson**

Just as in fact there can be no peace without order, so there
can be no order without justice. – **Pope Pius**

The final test of a leader is that he leaves behind him and
other men the conviction and the will to carry on.
– **Walter Lippmann**

There is no liberty but liberty on the law. Law does not
restrict liberty; it creates the only real liberty there is.
– **William Sumner**

Life is a test, this world a place of trial. Always the
problem, or it may be the same problem, will be presented to
every generation in different forms. – **Winston Churchill**

Limited in his nature, infinite in his desire, man is a fallen
God who remembers heaven.
– **Alphonse De Lamartine**

He's not the finest character that ever lived. But he is a
human being, a terrible thing is happening to him. So
attention must be paid. He is not to be allowed to fall into his
grave like an old dog. – **Arthur Miller**

He has seen but half the universe who never has been shown the House of Pain. – **Ralph Waldo Emerson**

The individual is foolish; the multitude, for the moment is foolish, when they act without the liberation; but the species is wise, and when the time is given to it, as a species it always acts right. – **Edmund Burke**

God grant me the serenity to accept the things I can't change, courage to change things I can and wisdom to know the difference. – **Reinhold Niebuhr**

Of all sad words of tongue or pen, the saddest are these: It might have been." – **John Greenleaf Whittier**

I have had sorrow … But I have born them ill. I have broken where I should have been. – **Charles Dickens**

Wise people, even though all laws were abolished, would still lead the same life. – **Aristophanes**

There were some who said that a man at the point of death was more free than all others, because that breaks every bond, and over the dead the united world has no power. – **Fenelon**

THE AFTERWORD

You know the old saying that what doesn't kill you makes your stronger. Well, I thought that I had been through the fire and the rain, and although it didn't kill me, I picked up some bumps and bruises along the way. I wish I had listened to my fallen comrades whose paths were ever so predictable. I should have listened to mom, who was ever so stern on me for staying out in the streets. I wish I had listened to pop when he told me to watch the streets and know when to walk away. I should have listened to the old-timers who were ever so convincing in saying that they had been there and done it all. I wish I had payed attention to the prisoners whose common sense was ever so common. I wish I had listened to the teachers who taught me lessons to be used in an environment which required skills. I should have listened to the preacher who prayed all his troubles away. I wish I had listened to friends who believed that true friends kept in touch and talked their problems out amongst each other. I should have listened to my children who love me unconditionally and always want me to be around. I wish I had listened to my wife whose prayers continuously blocked Satan's wrath, which hung over me at times like a pendulum. Last of all, I should have listened to the Almighty when I only saw one set of footprints, because I should have known then that the powers that be were from a book greater than me.

But like they say: **I almost got away!**

CLOSING DEDICATION

Hey Pop. I know you're saying, "I hope my oldest son is doing the right thing down there." You know that you taught me everything I know basically, so I can't stray too far to the right nor the left. I have one particular blessing that no one else has; you see, I was born to look like you. Every day of my life I have heard, "You look like your dad." I cherish that, so each morning that I look into the mirror, I see you; what a hell of a blessing that is. We're all missing you and thanking God for all the times that we shared. Mom is okay. We keep her laughing with those YouTube pranks. Although you're not around physically, we feel your presence occasionally. We often laugh and talk about you. We think of the many things that you would do in a particular situation.

I figured it out! A son should know what his father would do in certain situations; this would be his training from a boy to a man. I have always watched you, from fixing cars to fixing things around the house. I wasn't just keeping you company, I was learning. This is why, when it was time for you to go home, I said to you, "You have taught me all that you could; it's my time to teach now." It's called passing the torch and men have to pass it for generations to come. Although I never wanted this day to come, you welcomed it, so that I may one day teach your grandkids. I could never see as far as you!

Pop, I know you're sitting next to the Big Guy, leaning over and whispering in his ear, "My son's a good kid; watch over him, direct him and teach him your ways."

Hey Pop, remember the song we used to listen to that reminded you of your pop, Luther Vandross - "Dance with my Father." Now it's time to wish. I've listened to it several times recently and it knocked me to my knees, so give me a few before I can listen to it again.

I'm so sorry that I couldn't take this punch for you, but this came from a higher power. You know that I would've moved the world for you, but the same power that lifted you to the heavens, holds me in His hands. Like that old Christian song goes, "Save a seat for me." Good-bye for now!

I WILL LOVE YOU ALWAYS!!!

P.S. Don't worry about the Crew! I got them! And Willie Brown, I got him under my wing!

About the Author

Othir Brister, Jr. was born on the 1st day of August 1960 in Sunflower Mississippi; a state known for its hickory, oak woods, grain, super fertile soil, yielding soy beans, sweet potatoes, and other crops.

He was born to achievers Othir and Joann Brister who worked endless hours in cotton fields to ensure their children a better way of life. His parents set their eyes on moving to New York City; soon settling in the Big Apple with their three children. His mom opened up a Beauty Salon, and his pop became a Chef; a job he loved so dearly. Upon saving for a few years, they eventually brought a house in Queens, New York where the family expanded to three boys and two girls. There they all remained until the children began raising their own families. His Pop's heart gave out on him in July of 2018, which they all felt the effects of. So now, everyone stays close to mom making sure she's alright.

They say that a child's earlier years are their formative years. During Othir's earlier years he found that to be true. He watched his mom come from work while his pop headed out to work. So, he learned what work was about. His first job was that of a paper boy. It was an easy job; riding a bike, and throwing papers in yards, occasionally being chased by the neighbor's dogs-so much fun. The job ended when his mom found out that he was being ripped off by the owner. That was just the beginning of many jobs to come, and he had his share.

There were many sports that he was involved in, but basketball was his favorite. Basketball, friends, and the park was his life, along with the night lights. He only went home for one thing - to eat. The streets became his second home, so much that his family often went looking for him.

But, with all the good times, came the bad times. Before he could graduate from public school, a close friend was stabbed repeatedly in front of him during the graduation ceremony. Then, another was shot dead by a gang member. This left a scar!

In his high school days, he learned what team sports were about. He joined the track team with a number of guys from the neighborhood.

His speed increased earning him numerous awards: becoming fifth in the New York State Pentathlon, a Track Scholarship, and for the school a new recreational weight room. So, he set his sights on college. SUNY Farmingdale University was the number one track school at that time. The scholarship made it easy for him to get in. This college would set the blue print to the latter stages of his life. He would meet lifelong friends, and his wonderful soul mate, who he'd marry and have three children with. Inevitably, as a SUNY College, the two years were soon over. He later enrolled in Wagner College, then John Jay College and took special courses with Penn Foster College. He was introduced to a correctional environment as a summer job, while he was in college. Othir became a correctional counselor at Riker's Island Facility. After leaving college, he sought jobs in the correctional field.

He landed a job as a New York State Correctional Officer at Sing Sing Correctional Facility. He also worked: at Downstate Correctional Facility and Fishkill Correctional Facility.

After leaving the correctional field and wanting to remain in the law field, he became a Private Investigator. For numerous years he secretly watched people, their houses, tracked vehicles, located people, and listened to endless stories; a cycle that never changes.

But he can tell you this; he now has tremendous respect for all people; the poor, the incarcerated, the mentally challenged, and especially the so called normal.

DOWNSTATE CORRECTIONAL FACILITY

FISHSKILL CORRECTIONAL FACILITY

RIKERS CORRECTIONAL FACILITY

SING SING CORRECTIONAL FACILITY

www.ingramcontent.com/pod-product-compliance
Lightning Source LLC
Chambersburg PA
CBHW072016040426
42447CB00009B/1644